Our Betty

Our Betty

Scenes from my Life

LIZ SMITH

With illustrations by the author

SIMON & SCHUSTER

London · New York · Sydney · Toronto

A VIACOM COMPANY

With thanks to my editor, Angela Herlihy, for being so helpful.

First published in Great Britain by Simon & Schuster UK Ltd, 2006
A Viacom company

Copyright © 2006 by Liz Smith

1 3 5 7 9 10 8 6 4 2

www.simonsays.co.uk

Simon & Schuster Australia
Sydney

Simon & Schuster UK Ltd
Africa House
64-78 Kingsway
London WC2B 6AH

A CIP catalogue record for this book is
available from the British Library.

ISBN 0-7432-8533-6
EAN 9780743285339

Typeset in Palatino by M Rules
Printed and bound in Great Britain by
Mackays of Chatham plc, Chatham Kent

Contents

Our Betty

Beginnings

Our house was on the edge of town. At the back, there were long gardens with grim grey houses behind. At the front it was just open countryside, a flat treeless land, mostly allotments, with the Scunthorpe steelworks in the far distance.

From my bedroom window I could see into Miss Goy's garden. It was a big space with a sweeping wall going round the corner up into Normanby Road, which led to the steelworks. I would see Miss Goy walking slowly and drying her long, long hair, her head bent in a holy book.

She had a friend called Esme, and every Sunday they warbled hymns together at St George's church. Miss Goy upright; Esme leaning slightly towards her, fluttering her eyelids as she sang, the lashes heavy with white face powder. I used to sit behind them and wonder at their quivering notes.

They must have loved God because they didn't have time to turn and smile. In fact, all the years of my youth

I spent over the road, Miss Goy never spoke or said hello. Though it was a good job she loved God, because she went to him very early, and Esme was left to warble alone.

I returned to the same seat in church every Sunday. My Gran saw to that. And to the Sunday School, and to the Brownies. Anywhere, in fact, where I, a lonely isolated child, would be with children of my own age instead of being with her.

Losing my mother

They said I had a wonderful time with my mother. She had blue eyes and long golden hair, which she would dry galloping along on her pony Jack. She would tie me in the trap with a large scarf and trot out with me and make me laugh. She was stylish and loved colour and was very musical, they said.

But when I was two there was a new baby and I was sent to stay with a farmer relative. When I came back I rushed to the room to find the bed empty. They said I did not cry but stood a long time staring at the empty bed.

The baby died soon afterwards.

❀

So it came to pass that my mother's death in childbirth when she was twenty-three and I was two years old became the leading factor in the strangeness of my life. In an odd way it left me defenceless and I became particularly conscious of it when my father disappeared when I was seven. I lived with my grandparents.

I suppose it is an animal instinct that if there is no one standing beside you, others can push you around without fear of confrontation. This feeling seems to be found within families too, not only among strangers.

I remember going to visit my aunt with my father. I would have been around five years old. There were two girl cousins, one about my age and one a bit older. My greeting from the girls was to kick me around the ankles and crack my head against the door jamb because I could not spell Constantinople. I let out a piercing cry and a large egg shape appeared on my crown. Dad, asleep in an armchair, was furious when my cries woke him. His anger was directed against me, not the aggressors.

Ever since then I have sometimes felt the lack of some-one of my own to stand by me – a brother, a sister, a strong mother, someone who is on my side. I have missed my mother all my life and have spoken out loud to her frequently as I feel she is still near to me.

Hearth and home

Gran said, 'I can cook anything with feathers on except a shuttlecock.' So she could. And she did. She was a brilliant cook. To come into the kitchen from the freezing cold of a winter's day was heaven. Hot, newly baked bread filled the air with fragrance. Buns, cakes, pies, golden brown and delicious, baked in the iron oven at the side of the fire.

Often Grandad would have a glass of beer, thrust the poker into the fire, then, when it was red-hot, plunge it into the beer. It sizzled and flew, steamed and jumped. He called it mulled ale. I had some too, in my little glass. Whenever he drank I must drink with him, wherever he was I must be there.

The pantry was large and cool. On the floor stood earthenware jars of drinks: ginger beer, dandelion and burdock and lemonade all replaced each week by horse-and-cart delivery.

There was a fruit shelf; a huge dish held any fruit in season, always with a basket of apples at the side. High up on the top shelf were little jars, some with sheep's wool to stuff in our ears when they ached in the icy wind and goose grease to rub on to shivering chests. Not that Gran trusted this completely, for I always had to wear a piece of camphor in winter, strung around my neck in a little cotton bag, like a talisman against Jack Frost.

There was also a dark room off the pantry where fish sometimes gleamed with phosphorescent light on a

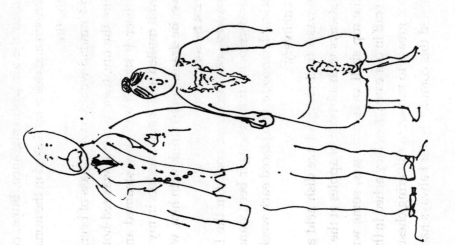

Grandma & Grandad.

marble slab. If Dad had been out with his gun there would be a hare hanging in the shadows, a paper bag over its head to catch the blood, and there would be game and pigeon pies for dinner.

Milk arrived at the back door by horse and trap. The milkman fished the required amount out of a large churn. A little bit of chat, a stroke of the horse's nose and exchanging a few coppers made it a little occasion. It was more fun than picking up a plastic bottle from a supermarket shelf.

On washing day the kitchen was a hive of activity. Mrs Hobson came to do the wash. The boiler was stoked up with a roaring fire, the water steamed and bubbled, bluebags were dipped into it to make the clothes whiter than white.

Huge zinc tubs were filled with soaking clothes or swished back and forth with a wooden clothes dolly, rubbed down a board for the dirty bits. Rinsed, then put through the mangle, turned by hand, and hung outside on the clothes line. God help us if it rained on Monday.

Mrs Hobson would take a mid-morning break. She would have a slab of homemade fruitcake, a piece of cheese and a glass of beer. I would keep her company with a beer in my small glass.

Ironing was done with flatirons heated on the fire. You picked one up with a cloth and spat on it to measure the heat and just kept changing one iron for another as they grew cold. What work, what hard work.

Off to the pictures

At home in Scunthorpe we had a tall, wind-up gramophone, and a piano which my mother had played very well. Once a week we went to the Palace Variety Theatre, but my real passion was the cinema, which we visited three or four times a week.

A little grey embroidered bag was filled with fruit and nuts to eat while watching Charlie Chaplin, Harold Lloyd, Laurel and Hardy, Tim McCoy, or whoever was showing. It must have been hell to sit near me, as I sucked oranges and cracked peanuts out of their shells, and, worst of all, because they were silent films, the dialogue had to be read aloud to me.

When *The Singing Fool* came out we were breathless with excitement. We charged up the cinema steps as Mr and Mrs Barley came down.

'Watzit like, watzit like? Can you really hear it?'

'Well, yes,' they said. 'You can hear it. But it's no good, it'll never last.'

Thank goodness it did. I grew up to go by myself and to love the music and colour of Bebe Daniels in *Rio Rita* and *Gold Diggers of Broadway*. Every Saturday matinée I was there, subsidized by the sale of flowers and mint out of the garden from a barrow, to see the candle burning through the rope that would send a huge boulder crashing on to the heroine below. Or the long-haired beauty tied to the railway tracks, as the train emerged from the tunnel and Jack the lad would rescue her just in time. Or the gallant hero falling from the high window of a burning building. But he made it, and by the next Saturday he had dropped and caught on to the windowsill of a lower window. 'Hooray!' we all cheered with delight.

Nora Travis took me to see the first *Frankenstein*. I wore my navy-blue coat with bell sleeves. But it was all too much for me and I passed out as Boris Karloff rose up from the table and gazed through the screen straight at me.

I woke in the foyer in a pale-green Lloyd Loom chair.

The Variety Theatre was fun. Most turns performed against a backdrop of a street scene with a barrow piled with fruit, lots of bananas. Acts were numbered at the side of the stage and framed by light-bulbs. Coarse comedians, magicians, glamorous singers, a line-up of lovely leg-swinging girls and, usually, an act consisting of a lady with a hard face and several excited dogs, hysterical with excitement to be let out of their cages.

Whenever there was an act with a gun, one of the lady attendants would come to Grandad and whisper in his ear, 'There's a gun in the next one, Mr Foster.'

He would always say, 'Take our Betty till it's over, then.'

The ladies had a box for their retiring room and there I sat with them in their black dresses and frilly white aprons, as a red velvet curtain cut out the sound of the action. We all ate chocolates.

Oh bliss. If only they would do that to me today. I hate explosions in theatres. If someone brings out a gun I sit screwed up and lose all the next dialogue.

Once a real play came to town. A group of strolling players brought *Uncle Tom's Cabin*. There was no theatre for them so they performed in the boxing ring below the railway lines. They were a family touring from town to town taking all their props and costumes in a woven skip.

Life must have been incredibly hard for those troupers in the 1920s.

Money must have been scarce, but we sat in the best seats and paid ninepence. The acting was wild and extravagant with many dramatic arm gestures. But it was from the heart and we cried a lot. Local children with blacked-up faces played extras, touching upon another world.

Baby Vickers comes to call

My wild father, Wilfred, would suddenly appear. Sometimes he lived with us. Sometimes he didn't. He travelled to faraway places a lot, like Leeds or Manchester. Always, he came back loaded with gifts for me. Jewellery and sweets. So I would sit in front of a roaring fire, drape myself in necklaces of crystal, diamante and pearls, and eat gargantuan amounts of toffees and chocolates.

'Let's go to the pictures,' Dad would cry, throwing me up into the air, so high I thought I would never come down. I screamed. Soon I was dressed in my latest outfit, a coat of rose-coloured cloth, fur tippet and white kid boots, and off we went to the cinema, not forgetting a bag of sweets.

Baby Vickers often came to call. She was blonde and beautiful and looked so cute with her Marcel wave. Her brief little dress of pale-green stockinet overchecked with black, and the long, long legs in pale-green silk stockings, strappy pale shoes with lavatory heels.

Oh lovely smiling Baby Vickers, I thought. I want Dad to marry you. I want you for my mother.

She brought her kid in a pram. The kid stood up and strained against the reins. I took a sharp intake of breath – she was wearing an ankle-length white fur coat. I was filled with envy.

I knew they were classy because they had fresh pineapple for tea. We only had tinned.

But although Baby wanted a husband, Dad didn't marry her. Alas, she faded out of our lives.

Sweets and dresses

My favourite shop was just over the road. It was tiny, dark, with a step worn away by generations of children's feet and a large brass bell on a spring which seemed to go on clanging for ever when it hit the door. This would bring Miss Tallentine out from the back parlour. She sailed into the shadowy shop like a warship defying the sea, her vast, jet-covered bosom thrusting towards the sweet jars.

My demands were brief – 'A ha'peth mixed' – as I handed over my halfpenny, then flung myself towards the paraffin bin. Climbing up on a ledge to the top of the big red bin I smelled and smelled paraffin, while Miss Tallentine solemnly screwed a square of newspaper into a cone, then went down the row of sweet jars taking one out of each until I had got my halfpenny worth. Coconut ice, cinder toffee, chocolate nougat, liquorice pipes, sugar mice, banana toffee …

She also had a wonderful lavatory at the bottom of her long garden. I had been there with a young visitor, and marvelled that it had a long seat, hanging over a cesspit, with four holes. There the whole family could start the day together. Squares of newspaper hung on a nail at either end, and the little building around the cesspit was completely covered with lichen, which seemed to sweeten the whole thing. Although there was a bucket of cinders with a shovel to sprinkle on the dirtier bits.

Bee's Ladies' Outfitters sold exclusive gowns. They had a special line of two-guinea dresses. Because you were paying this enormous price, a boy on a bicycle would ride up to your door with a large cardboard box containing a selection of dresses on approval. Then he would collect them when you had decided which one.

Miss Tallentie mixed me a ha'peth of sweets.

But Mr Bee had a brother with a small shop near me that Gran took me to a lot. She bought my Liberty bodices, combinations, and the incredibly thick fleece-lined knickers she felt would protect me against colds and the flu. It was that kind of shop. No large cardboard

13

boxes delivered to your door, but you were served personally by Selina Bee.

Although her mother owned the shop, Mrs Bee never served, but stood silently in the shadow of the doorway to the house. She was a tiny bird, a little bony frame and a huge, sharp nose like a beak. Eyes like blackcurrants and a tight slit of a mouth. She wore a dark gabardine dress with torn and dirty lace frills at the neck and wrists. She was crowned with a huge pile of silver hair, which fell untidily from a large, loose bun. As she stood watching, her fingers and mouth were never still; mouth puckering, fingers restlessly twisting the door curtain.

The shop was always in total chaos, torn curtains hung crazily, half drawn, across the dirty window. Stock years and years old was heaped up in a mad mountain, some in yellowed cardboard boxes spilling all over the place. It was said that behind the shop there was a large warehouse stacked high with boxes of goods going well back into the previous century.

Selina must have been about fifty years old. She had grey frizzy hair, a small-print cotton frock, and a faraway expression with a permanent smile. As she served, she constantly hummed a tuneless tune. Up would go the yardstick to measure the cotton luviska or flowered print, piled on top of a mountain of haberdashery, and up would go Selina's voice with it, quivering in a little song of no words. I cannot think of the horrors of life in that grim place. The father had long given up the ghost and hanged himself on the lavatory chain.

One day, turning the corner from Selina Bee's shop, I went down Mulgrave Street and found it different. It was covered end to end with horse manure. A woman was lying seriously ill in one of the houses there, and this was to give her peace and quiet.

Miss Judson had a dressmaking establishment in the High Street, with hairdressing on the ground floor. There I was taken at regular intervals to have my hair singed.

In the gloom of the shop the tapers flamed and gleamed up into the face of the girl as she ran them up and down the tight twists of hair. I sucked my knees in tight in case my head fell off, a burning ball. Then Gran might lift her hands in horror and be sorry she had brought me to Miss Judson's to have my hair singed. But Gran just smiled with pleasure as my hair was pulled back into ringlets.

Miss Judson descended the mahogany staircase at the back of the shop to escort us to the dressmaking department on the next floor. An awesome figure, she moved slowly. Her tall, thin body curving backwards, her arm held to balance a large ear trumpet, for Miss Judson was very deaf. This, of course, affected her voice, giving her

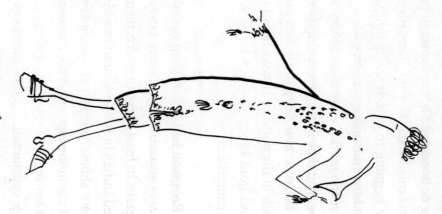

Miss Judson
The Dressmaker.

conversation a throaty, nasally tone, which only added to the mystery of her being.

Miss Judson always wore black satin. The longer-style dress of the twenties, mostly with double-length skirts with braiding or tassels and several rows of beads, some ending in pendants, nearly down to her knees.

'Our Betty is going to be a bridesmaid,' Gran spoke carefully into Miss Judson's ear trumpet.

'I huff joust the fabric,' came the throaty reply. 'This fine silk crêpe would be ideal for a spring wedding.'

We chose the pale blue. The dress had a long waist with three frills at the bottom, and we bought a goldleaf headband and gold brocade shoes to go with it. The shoes nearly caused a crisis.

Mr and Mrs Robinson had a shoe shop next door. It was cosy and always seemed to have a fire burning merrily away in the grate. In front of the fireplace, there was a rug showing a Red Indian in full-feathered headdress advertising moccasin shoes. At either end of the rug, an easy chair where I sat in the heat from the fire and had shoes slipped on to my feet.

Today, huge consternation, little squeaks of horror. Mr Robinson came rushing out of the storeroom. Mrs Robinson buried her face in her hands. Mr Robinson put more coal on the fire. Alas, my shoes were odd. On one shoe the brocade had a leaf pattern, the other had flowers. Apologies, apologies, return shoes. A matching pair arrived in time for the wedding.

It was Fanny Roper's wedding. She was marrying

Don, a detective in Hull. Fanny lived in Goxhill, a little village by the River Humber. She wore a long dress of white satin with a belt of diamonds. Real, I decided. The celebrations went on for days in the village hall.

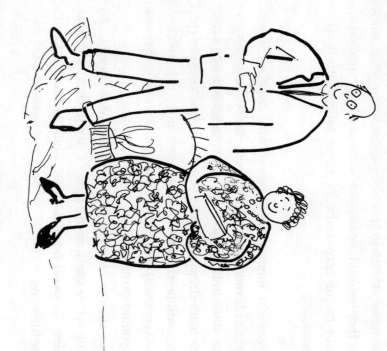

Hieronymus Robinson at the shoe shop.

I don't know how we travelled but we were met by a horse and trap. Gran rode with the driver and I flung myself down on the floor of the trap along with the wicker basket containing my precious blue silk dress and gold shoes. Someone dropped a couple of rugs over me, which put me into a dark woollen cave, then the horse started to trot. Ribble-rubble over the stones on that long flat road, I pressed my body against the floor of the trap and felt the journey every inch of the way.

My main memory of the wedding was seeing my Grandad, one hand on the bridegroom's shoulder and the other holding his best white handkerchief to catch the tears dropping on to his moustache as he begged, 'You will be good to her, won't you lad?'

'Aye, I will that, Mister Foster,' said the groom. And Grandad pushed his best hankie into his pocket, for it was alien to him. His daily hankie was a huge red one with white spots, made of very absorbent soft cotton to wipe the sweat from his brow when he stood in front of the furnaces.

Christmas

It snowed at Christmas, without fail. I always woke to a heap of toys that Father Christmas had left at the foot of my bed. I still have the little white teddy bear who sat there to greet me on Christmas morning 1924. He is white no longer and has lost his pretty pierrot hat but if you should squeeze him gently, he will still play you a pretty tune.

I had a lot of dolls and a doll's pram but preferred to have a dog sleeping in the pram. One of my favourite toys was the doll's house and I played with it endlessly. I loved the little furniture and the tiny potted plants with sticky glue bottoms to cling to the windowsills. And the little people who sat in the miniature chairs.

The sitting room was warm, and the fire made the wood surround smell sweet. I would stand in the bay window, by the aspidistra in its big glazed pot, and look at the snow falling in the street, and the Salvation Army band came round and played carols.

At the back of the room was the piano that I was told to practise on. I did less practise than play with the piano, and enjoyed lighting the candles and playing with the hot wax until one day I got it running so freely, it dripped on to the keys and, with the candle, set them alight.

Gran put her head around the door to see the piano all ablaze, yet all she said was, 'Oh, our Betty.' The blackened keys were left without any ivory on them. But soon after that, the visiting piano teacher rapped me over the knuckles with a pencil and got the sack. So I didn't continue to learn music and it is one of the big regrets of my life. If only I could have played just one instrument, my life would have been different. I could have joined in with others, made a little group. How I would have loved that.

When I was five years old I got engaged to a boy of the same age with a ring out of a Christmas cracker. I can't remember his name, but he sat with me on a doorstep smoking a penny clay pipe and vowed he would love me for ever. In the manner of all men. But how long is forever?

Street games

At that time my best friends were the gang of boys who played in the street – round and round in the garden barrow, and the bicycles and the hopscotch over the chalk lines on the pavements. And our flashlights that would shine red, yellow and green because then you could play safely in the street after dark.

The lamplighter would come round and light the gas lamps, and we would play around them. Somebody would bring a length of rope from their garden shed and make swings and maypoles with it in the green light of the gas and the yellow lamplight from Miss Tallentine's shop.

One night the boys grew sick of playing girlie things so decided to play hanging. They had the little victim strung up high on the lamppost with the rope around his neck. His face was turning blue and his tongue was hanging out. Looking up, the boys gathered around him and said, 'Whistle when tha's had enough.' It was lucky that a grown-up passed by at that moment and stopped play.

I can only remember one girl I played with at that time – her name was Connie Green and I was horrid to her. I remember sitting on the hearth rug in front of the fire in a darkened room, putting on a leather glove and telling her I was going to turn as brown as the glove and I would very soon be a monster.

I *was* a monster. The poor girl spent all night running round the house calling for help. I didn't see much of her.

But there were birthday parties and the boy next door had lovely ones with lots of jellies and cakes. At the side of the loaded table was the radio and we all listened to *Children's Hour*, with Larry the Lamb and Uncle Mac, and the high spot of the whole party was when they read out the birthday names. When they read out the name of our birthday boy we all went wild. It did not happen for me because at that time we did not have anything as advanced as a radio, only the piano and the wind-up gramophone.

I did have a little party to mark my birthday, and that meant a visit to the potted-meat man. He lived in the pretty cottage at the bottom of Mulgrave Street, and when you were having any kind of a do, you ordered the potted meat from him which he delivered in an enamel dish.

Once I went to order some potted meat and he told me his little girl was ill in bed, and would I go up and see her. Of course I knew her, as in a town like that, everybody knows everybody. As I entered, I was struck by the darkness of the room. Her bed was in deep shadows. There was one tiny window way up in the wall and it struck me then that all those pretty postcard whitewashed cottages were not so much fun to live in.

Next door to the potted-meat man was a square piece of ground, asphalted and surrounded by a fence. In the centre stood a gypsy caravan, highly decorated and richly rococo, where lived Mr Jacklin with his wife and two daughters.

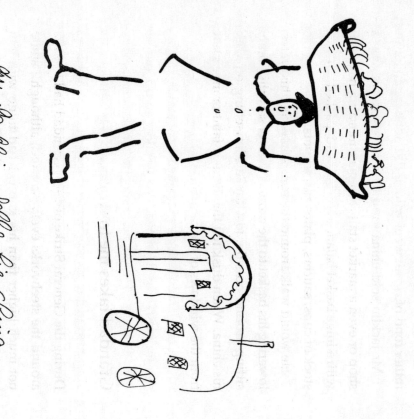

Mr Jacklin sells his china.

Mr Jacklin was of Romany blood. He had been given this piece of freehold land by a local landowner for his bravery in the 1914 war when, I believe, he won the VC. His story fascinated me and I used to watch the caravan as I passed on my way to Selina Bee's or Mrs Dixon's shop on the corner, which sold a little savoury pie I was rather fond of.

Mr Jacklin sold china for a living. He did not own a shop or even a market stall but every morning he set off with a huge basket balanced on his head, packed with his stock of cups, saucers, plates and teapots.

He would walk around the streets hawking his wares, lowering his basket to the ground. I never saw the family sitting around outside, just Mr Jacklin setting off with his china. When dusk fell there was a faint orange glow from the windows of the caravan.

Grandad takes me to work

During the General Strike of 1926, Grandad had to walk around the steelworks every day and, although I stood not much higher than his knees, I had to go with him because he was my hero.

The works had that strange otherworldly feeling

empty places have when they are normally filled with people and movement. They were vast. As big as the world, they seemed to me. Huge cubist structures in shades of grey, shot with shafts of pale mote-filled light.

We usually had a couple of dogs with us. They were our safeguards. As we walked along the platforms, if the dogs leaped, it meant a plate was missing. Not to notice would have meant a sixty-foot drop to the rolling mills below.

But that was an image soon gone. Came the days when the works were roaring again and I could take Grandad his dinner between two plates. The only thing I remember him eating is oxtail and cabbage.

Once again the steel was boiling in the great vats, the orange glow like any picture of hell. The workers would let it cool then take a sample on a long, long pole, grind it to dust and bring the result to Grandad, who would direct them to bring a bit of this or that – like, for instance, a few tons of iron ore. This went on until he was satisfied and then, when the steel was ready, the drama started. The men, stripped to the waist and gleaming with sweat, lined up holding a battering ram. Everyone was instructed to wear dark-blue or green glasses. Then Grandad said, 'Come on me lads', and with groans like slaves they swung the ram at the furnace until it burst.

It was pure theatre. Out poured the stuff like a volcano and fell into a bucket to be carted off to the rolling mills. If a man fell in he would melt long before he met the molten metal.

Come to think of it, I doubt if a child of four or five years old would be allowed to stand there in her dark-blue glasses today.

Raining cats

It was a grey day. I decided to go for a walk, but because it was spitting rain I tore off a large stick of rhubarb. Up I went on the grim, flat Normanby Road, a sullen dyke beyond the pavement littered with cans, bottles and the occasional dead dog.

It grew darker. In the distance the steelworks made a jagged outline against the sky, an occasional orange flame burst from the tall chimneys. The landscape was grim and empty, but slowly a little figure materialized, stood before me.

'It's raining,' I said.

'I know.'

'You can come under my rhubarb leaf if you like.' Heads together, we walked back to my garden.

'What's your name?'

'Tilly.'

'You can have a go on my swing.'

Then this kitten arrived. I'd never had a kitten, as here they were regarded as vermin. Mrs Thompson on the corner kept a gun handy, ready to shoot any cat daring to come into her garden.

Tilly liked the swing, and the kitten. I thought the kitten might like a swing, but I couldn't work out how to hold it and the ropes. The obvious answer was to put it in my thick knickers from Selina Bee. I hoped it was having a good time, until it was very sick in there.

I didn't see Tilly or the kitten again. A pity, because not many people I feel to be my soulmate.

Plough Jags

The night of the Plough Jags was strange. They came in late spring when the nights were warm enough to go out without a coat. People came round the corner by Mrs Thompson's house. All sorts of people I had never seen before, strangers. It was all a bit shadowy and smoky. I think someone had let off some fireworks and the light from the gas lamp in the street was slightly green.

The crowd gathered in untidy groups. They were mostly men in shabby clothes, probably farm labourers, as it was a hiring night, when they would get a job to work on a farm for a few shillings a week for another year.

Mrs Williams watched them from her bed. She pressed her face against the window and looked down. I saw the whiteness of her nightie. Gran said she was in bed with a woman's thing, and when Gran twisted her face as she said it, you knew it was something not to be spoken of.

The high spot of the evening was when the morris dancers came down and into our midst. Backwards and forwards they danced in the flickering gaslight, waving ribbons. They were trimmed with flowers and had a lot of bells all over them, just like Jack, our horse, had worn. And their big feet lifted up and slammed down to the strange music they played and they banged big sticks to the rhythm.

And somewhere in the crowd were the Plough Jags, who were local players. The atmosphere became a bit weird and threatening so I sped up the ten foot between the houses, back to Gran's warm fireside – and, no doubt, cake with treacle.

The Zam-Buk shop

When I was a child, I only ever saw one black man. He was the husband of the lady who kept the Zam-Buk shop.

The Zam-Buk shop was next to Selina Bee's drapery shop and it was a routine progress, after buying my thick winceyette knickers and combinations, to call in for some Zam-Buk ointment to rub on my knees in case I should fall over.

The shop had a dreamlike quality. Everything about it was in soft ochre colours, fading from dark to light. The grooved wooden walls were covered in ancient paint that had acquired a patina like yellow-tinged smoke.

When the shopkeeper glided into view behind the counter, it was hard to distinguish the difference between her colours and the wall. Her soft cotton garments were of the same earth colours, and her face emerged gently: the face of a saint, as seen on a faded fresco.

There were stretches of empty counter and display

shelves, except for an occasional isolated tin of Zam-Buk ointment. There was nothing else to ask for, as far as I could see.

But behind that pale shop, she had a new husband. A giant of a man. Black until he shone blue, with tribal scars on his cheeks which marked him out to be a prince in a far-off land.

I would see him escorting her tenderly down Mulgrave Street – her, like a pale shadow by his side. She said that he was the most wonderful, caring, dearest husband in the world and not to be compared to the self-ish, indifferent one she had had years ago.

Then, when I was seven, I saw Al Jolson in *The Singing Fool*. But I guessed that was black paint.

Sherbet dabs

Grandad had an open touring car and on a summer's evening would take us for a drive. Gran buttoned up my coat. She gave me half a crown (thirty old pence).

'Betty, I want a cauliflower for tomorrow. Go up to Silly Billy's and get one before we set off.'

Silly Billy couldn't do a lot but he could grow

vegetables, which he sold for a living, but this evening he didn't have a cauliflower.

Here I was, in possession of half a crown, and nothing to spend it on. Quick as a flash I was over the worn step of the sweet shop and had handed over the money. Because they were only a halfpenny each, I got sixty sherbet dabs and suckers.

When Grandad saw what I had done, he pulled on his leather helmet and driving goggles and groaned, 'Oh Betty.'

I sat next to him on the front seat with the deliciously loaded cardboard box on my lap. In my eagerness I ripped the packets open rapidly.

It was a pleasant evening with a stiff breeze, and by the time we returned I had sampled all sixty of the dabs and suckers. Grandad sat there like a white statue, covered in sherbet with just enough rubbed off his goggles to drive us home. He and Gran never said a word, just cleaned off the mess.

What fun I had, sharing time with Grandad. The winter nights when I sat with him in front of the fire, when he would tell me the rules of life as we ate. Whole raw onions cut into thin slices, or sections of grapefruit. Best of all, Gran's hot oven-bottom cakes, torn open and thick with butter and syrup.

'Now listen, Betty. There's an answer to everything. You just have to look for it.' Or, 'When you're out with the horse and trap, never hand your horse to the hosteler to put up for the night. Do it yourself. Have an old sheet with you and bind his legs with cow dung. He'll be in fine fettle next morning.'

Advice I have never had to take. Alas.

First day at school

Gran took me along to my first day at school in my pushchair. It was a large wooden box shape with a flap at the front for climbing in through. I curled up on the floor wrapped in a rug, and travelled in darkness. When we arrived the flap was thrown back and I emerged, to be greeted by my new teacher.

She was a tall and beautiful blonde, wearing a dress of the most colourful fabric I had ever seen. It was a shift made of velvet from Liberty's, colour upon colour upon colour. It was imprinted on my mind for ever. She was a bored wife who had opened this little kindergarten school to keep herself amused.

Each day, for me, was just happiness. There was no discipline whatsoever, which was heaven at the time, but

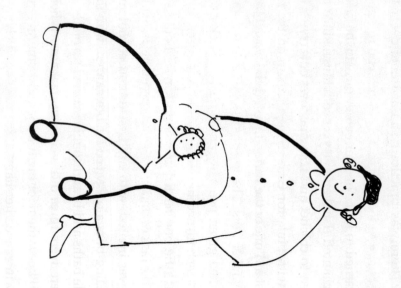

First play at school.

hell for me later in my life when I had to conform. I had to read and write early because we were always writing stories and poems.

Then, drawing the pictures to attach to the poems, then acting them out with movement and maybe a little song. There was practically no arithmetic – that was dull.

I learned to knit. 'In over, under off,' the blonde goddess chanted. I haven't advanced a stitch since then. I learned to crochet and trimmed a set of terry-towelling mats with pink, for Gran. She put them on the marble washstand under the water jugs and the wash bowl and the chamber pots. The pot that stood on the floor often contained green pee as Gran had a bad back and took pills, which turned her water bright jade green.

The little boy next door went to my school so I was given the task of undoing the buttons on his leggings. For this I was invited, with Gran, to his house. He lived in a sprawling bungalow set in a large garden, with sunken marble baths and beautiful rooms.

There were three older children from an earlier marriage. I knew them for being poorly dressed, and in bitter cold winter weather having no socks or stockings, only heavy boots. Two of them were girls.

To get to the handsome drawing room we had to walk through the kitchen where the three older children sat at a rough wooden table eating bread and margarine, wearing their clumsy boots on their spindly legs.

In the drawing room, their stepmother sat with her pet monkey on her shoulder and a toilet roll always at the ready. We had food on a lace-covered table with a centrepiece of electric-light tulips. After we had eaten, we were entertained by Mr and Mrs. She played the grand piano, and he the saxophone, very well indeed as I remember.

But although people had glimpsed these poor children of a former wife rushing around with their legs bare, emptying cinders and making up the fires before they went to school, no one tried to stop it. I just kept on helping my schoolmate off with his beautiful soft, warm clothing.

Great-grandfather Jonathan

Across the road from our house was a little white cottage where my great-grandfather Jonathan lived. He was the Lincolnshire one, so came from a different race of people. The grandparents I lived with, my mother's parents, were true Yorkshire. Grandad had been sent from the steelworks in Sheffield to the new steelworks in Scunthorpe during the 1914–18 war.

My father and his family were all from Lincolnshire. The two counties bordered each other, but to me it was a total conflict of character. Everything warm, real and life-giving came from Yorkshire. Everything mean and colourless came from Lincolnshire.

Great-grandfather Jonathan was an old man of great respectability and had lived in that cottage all his life. When he was a child, he had planted the core of an apple he had just eaten and the result was a tree growing at the side of the house with the most delicious apples I had ever tasted.

In the spring that piece of ground was a sea of blue, with the bluebells. When the apple blossom was out, it was a sight to take my breath away when I peered through the white picket fence. And was even more beautiful when I thought how all that lovely blossom would mean a good crop of apples this year.

I passed Great-grandfather Jonathan's house whenever I went to Miss Tallentine's sweet shop. Which meant I passed it quite often. Sticking my nose through the fence, I kept my eye on the growing apples and as soon as they were big enough I was over the road with a little woven basket. Great-grandfather Jonathan would give me some of the apples, but always expected me to give him three pennies for them, which was quite a lot of money at that time.

It was the same with the firewood. He had a large woodyard further up the village surrounded by sheds packed with tree trunks. In the centre of the yard was a platform, where stood a gigantic circular saw with teeth like dragons', and when a tree was pushed on to it, it hit the saw with a scream. I would stand in one corner and wait for the wood to hit the saw and watch the great wave of sawdust fly up, then fall to the ground. Then I would bring our garden trolley and ask for the bits of wood that were on the ground for kindling for the fires at home. Great-grandfather Jonathan filled my little barrow with the wooden bits, but again he charged me three pennies.

I remember once, when we still had the car and were on our evening tour, we called in to see his daughter who would have been my Great-aunt Hetty. She was married to a farmer with several farms. In fact, her house was where my mother's horse Jack had been sent to live when my mother died.

We used to stop at the field where Jack lived and call him to the gate, and he would come running with a whinny and we would stroke him and kiss his nose.

After seeing Jack we would go to the house for a social visit and there would be a cup of tea in a beautiful china cup. One evening, Great-aunt had made some jam tarts. They were delicious. I ate mine quickly and asked if I could have another one.

Though it is eighty years ago I can still see the

expression on Great-aunt's face. She sat bolt upright in her white silk blouse with a cameo brooch at the neck, her face rosy with disapproval, her mouth slightly sagging open. Silently, she offered the plate for me to take another one.

It was exactly like Oliver Twist asking for more gruel.

So it was that very early in my life I decided the Lincolnshire ones were mean.

Because Great-grandfather Jonathan had only three daughters and no sons to inherit the woodyard, he decided to sell it. George, who worked for him, bought it, and straight away closed it and used all the trees to make coffins.

George had two sons, and sent them off to learn embalming. He also bought a very large Rolls-Royce. Now, embalming was just becoming a very fashionable thing, and very soon he was doing a roaring trade. Not only did the departed loved ones look all pink and healthy, but the family got to ride behind the hearse in a large Rolls-Royce, past all the neighbours' houses at a time when hardly anybody had a car.

The garden party

Dad swept into the house like a whirlwind as usual. This time it was not to take me to a film. There was a garden party in the grounds of a big mansion just outside the town. So I must go with him, I must look my prettiest and he would be so proud of me. Everyone would be there, crowds and crowds of people.

Gran worked at speed. Off came my fleecy lined heavyweight knickers, on went a delicate pair in white silk with frills on. A dress of white broderie anglaise, pale-blue ribbon trim and hair ties, pale-blue shoes. Dad was thrilled. So off we went. Together.

It was a brilliant hot summer's day, the lawns were crowded. Dad held my hand and took me amongst the people. Until he spotted someone he wanted to be with even more. Quick as a flash he looked around.

We moved even quicker through the crowd. This was fun. It got more and more frantic. He stopped before someone he seemed to know and said something softly in their ear. They nodded.

Swiftly, they took hold of my hand, and even more swiftly Dad had disappeared into the crowd. They brought me home. It was a small town, so everyone knew everyone and where they lived.

Night came and I went to bed. Apparently, in the middle of the night there was a tremendous knocking on the door. When Gran and Grandad crept downstairs (no doubt with a poker), they found Dad on the doorstep, dead drunk and covered with his own vomit.

Leaning against the wall, he lifted his head and said, 'I've given our Betty away.' He couldn't believe I was in the house and couldn't remember who he had given me to. That was how I came to be woken at 3 a.m. to be taken down to show him I was there in the flesh.

I came into the room to find Dad lying paralytic across the sofa, stinking of the vomit that spilled down his suit. He looked up at me with heavy-lidded eyes. After a long pause, he said, 'Some bugger's been sick down me.'

Summer days

There was a golden glow over that period of my childhood. The summers were long and hot. Cornfields where the wheat was pulled into wigwam shapes and smelled hot in the sun; a stream edged with kingcups, forget-me-nots and cowslips; hedges with butterflies darting in and out, wild roses, elderflowers.

There was a bus standing in my garden, which Grandad had bought for my playhouse. I caught little fishes in the stream with my net and had them in a bowl on my playhouse table; I never understood why they died so soon – upside down they turned, one by one, stiff little silver streaks. I scattered them outside on to the graves of my dead dogs.

The dogs I loved so much that I often had two or three sleep on my bed, sometimes would die or be killed on the road. When this huge tragedy happened they were given a grave in the playhouse garden, a cross (for were they not Christian?) with their name on.

Gardens were wild, real, tangled masses of flowers and grasses. Except, of course, that of Mrs Thompson who just had huge, smooth lawns so she could see a cat coming a mile away and get a better aim with her gun. At the bottom of every garden was a shed; this was where we often played.

Layers and layers of old wallpaper lined the walls, remains of a bedroom decoration of twenty years before, a front parlour from last year. All dampened in the bitter winter wet and now dried out in the hot sun to a papier mâché crust, smelling of mould, mushrooms and roses.

There we would gather and if, by any chance, a boy

joined us, he might give us a quick glimpse of his four-year-old willie. Then the girls would scream and fling themselves against the walls of the shed.

Another trick for the girls was peeing through their knickers. This was done in a tribal way, squatting around in a circle. Not forgetting that in the 1920s, knickers were often buttoned-on things made of very fine cotton. I fancied this and joined the circle. The others peed straight through their thin underwear, but I had forgotten that I was wearing Gran's fleecy-lined knickers from Selina Bee's, and they simply filled up with liquid. Those knickers, my woollen combinations and Liberty bodices were the bane of my life.

Grandad's plans

Grandad said to Gran, 'Liza, I have got to think about you and our Betty if anything should happen to me.'

'Nothing will happen to you Bob,' said Eliza.

But of course, it did. He was swept away in the flu epidemic of 1930. Yet at this point he had plans. He knew that, because he paid no National Insurance, there would be no widow's pension for Eliza if he should die.

So, along with three other men in a similar position, it

was agreed that they would each contribute one thousand pounds to form a bus company. This seemed a pretty good idea because the steel town was surrounded by little villages left over from its agricultural past, but with no way of getting in to the shops. The only wheels people had were on bicycles. It was a sure winner.

So it was settled, and Grandad felt assured that Gran would have an income if he died. The plans for the bus company were going ahead.

One day I was lying on the curly sheepskin rug that Uncle Billy had given Dad for a wedding present. It was nice to lie on it, eat sweets and hear the logs crackle. Our living room had been papered a lovely terracotta colour with a gold vein. I liked that.

There was a knock on the front door. I went to answer it. Behind the squares of coloured frosted glass I saw the dark shadow of a man and, waist high, a blob of yellow. It was Dad.

He was carrying a few daffodils, which looked as if they had been grabbed from somebody's garden. Head bent, he stood in a dramatic pose, then held out the daffodils towards me.

'Hello kid. These are for your mother's photo,' he said. Gran carefully arranged the flowers in the silver vase which always stood by my mother's photograph.

He managed to cross the hall and slump into the chair by the sideboard, leaning his head on his arm to tell his sad tale. Grandad stood and listened. It was the same story. Money, serious debts, bankruptcy. Nowhere to turn. Help. Help.

Still standing in the middle of the room, Grandad explained the present state of things, how he was investing his thousand pounds in the bus company for our security.

'But what,' he said, 'would happen to Liza and our Betty if I died? If I gave you the money instead, would you look after them?'

Tears ran down Dad's face.

'Oh, I will, I will care for them, I will look after them. Depend on me – I promise.'

His head sank lower. He sobbed. He cried and cried. The tears poured down. Grandad gave him the money. Dad needed the car as well. He got it.

Farewell Dad

I was seven years old. It was a hot summer's day, a Sunday. So of course I was sent to Sunday School. I was wearing a pale-turquoise coat and large brimmed straw hat. I was pleased to be looking pretty because, when I got outside the church, Dad was waiting for me.

He stood with his back to the sun. It shone in my eyes. I was glad of the wide brim. He wore a brown pinstriped suit and two-tone shoes; his black hair was very crinkly.

'Hello kid,' he said.

'Hello Dad.'

'I'm going away for a little while, kid. But I will write to you.'

'OK Dad.'

He lifted his right arm in a salute against the sun and started walking slowly backwards.

'I'll write kid. I'll write.'

He never did. Never.

For five years, I waited in the bay window playing the wind-up gramophone and watching the garden path in case the postman should walk up there at any old time. Playing all the songs and swing music of the 1920s, I waited and watched until I went to big school. I recall Henry Roy and his orchestra, with 'Tiptoe Through the Tulips', 'London Bridge is Broken Down' and 'Charmaine'. Also, John McCormack singing his melancholy songs, which suited my mood.

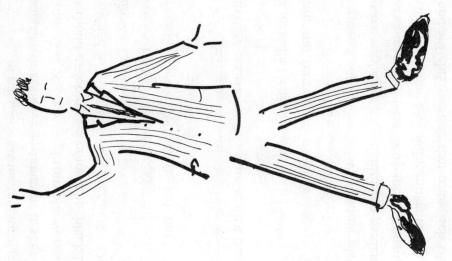

'Bye, bye,' said Dad,
in his two-tone shoes.

'Oh, the days of the Kerry dances,
oh for the ring of the piper's tune,
gone alas like our youth too soon.'

Or the sad song about the old house and the children all gone. I listened to them over and over again. Over and over again.

But from Dad, I had not even a postcard.

Adopted by Gran

After Grandad died in the flu epidemic, I had to leave my easy-going, dreamy pretend school and go to the local big school. It was a terrible shock – for the first time I met with discipline.

We became very poor. We had the house, but there was no widow's pension for Gran, only her savings to live on. Dad never sent a penny towards my keep. Remembering the neighbour's children and their little legs blue with cold in their big boots and no socks, Gran decided to adopt me. In case, she said, Dad claimed me to slave for a new wife.

So she added her name to mine and we went to the Magistrates' Court to do it.

There was a woman there who had been beaten by her husband until her breasts were black. She had to show them to the court, which shocked Gran.

'She had to show her bresses.'

Gran would deliberately mispronounce words that were too delicate, like 'God', which was difficult to say out loud, so she said 'Gord', as it was more respectful.

I wore a navy-blue serge coat that day.

A new joy

The elocution class had started putting on little plays and was willing to perform them for suitable charities. This usually happened in a church hall, in aid of the roof fund, or the bell fund or whatever. My first part was as a cook, about fifty years old, in a one-act play called *Between the Soup and the Savoury*, when I was nine. I took a little bag of flour to the hall to scatter all over my arms.

But for lighter moments, in the Christmas show, I made a wild dress from cotton scraps and made the people laugh and laugh. Oh how they laughed. I got sillier and sillier and the laughter rose to a shriek and the lights shone and shone, lots of electric lights – all shining.

That was it. That was what I wanted to do with my life. Make people laugh, have lots of lights, no gloom and no oil lamps.

Mrs Sellick

'She won't stand the ghost of a chance,' said the sour headmistress to Gran, knowing I had come from that no-good school. Of course I couldn't get to the grammar school, because I couldn't spell or do maths.

What a relief. I didn't want the grammar school. I wanted the other one, where the well known Mrs Sellick taught. I got there – and she was my inspiration. Once again, a goddess with a range stretching far outside our little domain. Not a tall, golden goddess this time, but an older, dark-haired woman of vast proportions. She taught art and drama, my two loves. And she brought me a feeling of a wider world beyond our narrow provincial town.

In the English classes we read the tales of Boccaccio, including 'The Monkey's Paw', and for the school show they hired the Variety Theatre, where I had sat only a few years ago with the ladies in frilly white aprons, behind the red velvet curtains when there was a gun in the act. There was no gun in the school act, only magic.

Mrs Sellick chose *The Last Days of Pompeii*, which she directed in a spectacular way. The Roman robes were swathes of fine white cotton edged with designs we painted on in the art room. What with the words, the movement, the fabric-painting, it was bliss.

They didn't mind that I was no good at games, or that my arithmetic was no good either. They welcomed what I *could* do, and I wallowed in it. I was so happy at that school.

It didn't bother me that I had to be on time. I wanted to be on time. I couldn't wait to get there and away from my sad, dark house where Gran sat in the light of an oil lamp and cried and cried to go to Grandad. I went willingly down the Normanby Road, under the trees and past the lovely gardens to a world where I belonged. Chiefly because of Mrs Sellick.

Gran still made all the bread and cakes, though on a much smaller scale. There were no more feasts of game, and the big jars of ginger pop and the sarsaparilla dried up. But food was always first priority because, as Gran said, you did not have good health without good food, and health is number one.

She sat solemnly in the lamplight and told me over and over again, 'When I'm gone, Betty, you will be completely alone. No one will care about you. I will try and live until you are twenty. I will try and leave you some money. With this money you must buy a house and it will be your safeguard in case you have a husband who leaves you. He must be the one to go and you remain in the house, which will protect you.'

This was her command, which she repeated again and again.

My bicycle

Grandad had had a bicycle specially made for my seventh birthday. It was built a bit big so it would last, and I started with wooden blocks on the pedals. There was very little traffic on the roads and I cycled everywhere.

By the time I was sixteen, the wooden blocks had long gone, my legs, much grown, spindled out at an angle, and the now little bike clattered and squeaked and clanged as its various parts moved painfully.

Grandad had been dead a long time, and there was no money now. The gallant little wreck still carried me around, and this was how I discovered I would never be able to drive a car.

I've always had dreams – unfortunately, I go deep into

them and lose sight of my surroundings. One particular day, I was jolted out of my daydream to find myself on a furious teacher's feet. I'd walked right into her but never saw her because of where my mind was.

It was the same thing this time. I had set off up the long flat road towards the steelworks. There I was, on the wreck, lost in one of my dreams. Sailing along in a fairy palace and oblivious to the world. I suddenly woke to confront several hundred screaming men, also on bicycles.

Not surprisingly, I was the object of their fury. It was the end of the shift at the steelworks and in my unconscious state I had peddled slap into the first few coming out. The rest had rapidly built up behind. All I saw were hundreds of open mouths with a lot of noise coming out of them.

The last incident with my bicycle was when I was deflowered outside Woolworth's. The bike, by this time, was all shifting parts. The saddle had fallen backwards, point upwards, though I hadn't noticed as by now I was tall enough to ride standing up. But one day when the lights changed abruptly, I braked abruptly – and, even more abruptly, sat heavily on the upturned saddle.

Wow!

Dressmaking

In the late 1930s it seemed that, if you were a girl, you could choose to learn typing and shorthand then work in an office, be a nurse, or, if you were very bright, a teacher. Well, I didn't fit any of those things. It was such a worry how I would earn my daily bread, come the day Gran had gone.

So, when I was sixteen she sent me to learn to sew with a dressmaker called Olive. It was quite an eccentric set-up. There was a workroom in the top back bedroom of the Victorian house and a reception room for the clients in the front. I was up and down the stairs because I had to entertain the customers and help them to choose their outfits from the endless pattern books. I had to wear a yellow embroidered smock and spent many happy hours with my legs hanging over a chair while the five-shillings-a-week maid mended the ladders in my stockings and told me of her love life. Lots of people then had a five-shillings-a-week maid who worked like a slave. Some even shared one with a friend.

I didn't mind how long I spent in the reception room with the ladies and the pattern books because I found it fascinating. It was quite a dim, heavily curtained room, thickly carpeted wall to wall in a deep, vibrant purple.

As a child in Scunthorpe

Marrying JT in 1945

My mother with her pony, Jack, 1916

Sarah's wedding to Ron, 1973

In the WRENS

Robert and Sara's wedding, 1985

Hard Labour, in which I played a woman who worked for others

With Ed Wilson in
Geordie's Court in 1975

The Brandon family of *I Didn't Know You Cared* in Sheffield, 1975

Dressed for *Within These Walls* in 1978

Peter Sellers was most amused at my nose when I played Madam Balls in two of the Pink Panther movies

With Yootha Joyce in *Bird Alone* which was never broadcast

Enjoying *Russ Abbot's Madhouse*, 1980

As Maggie Smith's dumb old mum in *A Private Function*

Playing Peter O'Toole's mother in *High Spirits*

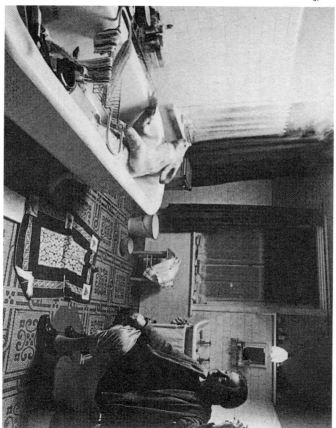

The gruesome photograph from *A Private Function* that did not make it into the film

There was a grand piano and quite a few palm trees. They were artificial; Olive had sent for them from a shop in London called Gamages.

Talk about exotic! There wasn't another front room like that anywhere in the street.

Miss Bush, the chimney-sweep's daughter, was getting married; maybe she was influenced by the colour of the carpet, because she chose deep purple for her bridesmaids' dresses. All eight of them in full-length crinolines – layer upon layer of violet-coloured net, like *Come Dancing* dresses. Mr Bush was such a tiny little man, ingrained with soot. He must have looked a bit overwhelmed by the eight purple crinolines as he escorted his daughter up the aisle.

Olive was perhaps in her late forties. She had been engaged for nearly twenty years and sometimes her reluctant suitor would call. Then there might be a little party, when she would sit at the piano and sing with great energy. Her favourite song was 'I love me, I love me. I love sweet little me.'

Whenever we were not sewing for others, we were set to make and trim her beautiful pure silk satin underwear and nightwear, all to be stowed away in chests. Drawers and drawers of the most beautiful silken things awaiting the dreamt-of wedding night. I don't think it ever came. I never heard anything about it.

Gran now wanted me to sew properly, so had found me a place in the workroom of Herbert Clayton's Fabric Emporium. Here I found myself at a long brown lino-covered table actually putting bits together until they became a dress or skirt. I wasn't keen to be early. I went on the old battered bike, and poor Herbert's face exploded into bright crimson balloons when he caught me creeping in through the back door.

Blaze away

I hadn't been at Herbert's very long – in fact, I had just got to be trusted with putting one seam to another – when down in the high street they put up a trestle table. It was early spring, 1939. The weather was mild and the windows were open. Some rather important-looking people were sorting out leaflets, putting them in neat piles on the tabletop.

Army, Navy, Airforce.

They fixed up a gramophone with electric sound, so you could hear it from one end of the street to the other. They had only one record, 'Blaze Away', which played all day. Da . . . de . . . da . . . da . . . de . . . da. We crept to the open window and left the sewing on the table, to watch the crowd in the street and listen to the uniformed people telling them all the advantages of Army, Navy, Airforce.

So it drifted on until one Sunday morning in September. I was having a late breakfast because it was my lie-in day, when Mr Chamberlain came on the wireless and said we were at war. I thought we were to be bombed immediately. I flung myself on my knees and asked God to forgive me for not being in church and please, please not to bomb me because I couldn't stand bangs.

I studied the uniforms and decided the smartest was the Navy one. So I joined the WRENS, while I still had a choice. If you didn't volunteer you were called up and had to go and do whatever they said. So here I was, accepted for the WRENS, and looked forward to sea and ships.

But instead, I got aeroplanes in the Fleet Air Arm.

Gran sees me off

In early 1940 I had received my calling-up papers and was off to the war. We knew the war out there was spreading and we felt the whole world was against us.

57

We did not know what was happening or who would be our enemy.

Everywhere it was rumour and speculation about what might happen to us. At the top of our fears was Hitler's secret weapon. What was it? Nobody knew. Everyday it was something different. The feeling was terrifying and vast, yet unknown. In those days, don't forget, we had no television to give us an up-to-date account and not everyone had a radio.

The streets were dark, as no lights were allowed. Windows were draped in black curtains. Here and there on the pavement there was a low blue light to show the way.

So I was going out into the world. Gran took me to the station. She thought for a bit, then said, 'Always make sure your vest is aired.' They must have been her last words to me.

Reporting for duty

I had to report to Greenwich. Crossing London to get there caused me so much anguish my period came on. I was overcome by the sight of the glorious painted hall.

I was standing at the back, with the amazing ceiling above me, and stretching as far as the eye could see was row upon row of teenaged sailors, new recruits newly shorn and with blue and white sailor collars. They were so young and their necks were so thin.

We danced and danced in the hangers to all the tunes of the forties – Joe Loss's music. I loved ballroom dancing. The soldiers from the nearby camps were Czechs, Poles, and there were sailors and airforce. The Americans had not yet arrived. Every unit seemed to produce a band and the music was wonderful.

Then we climbed back into the canvas-covered lorries and went back to quarters.

I was sent to Eastleigh in Hampshire and learned how to pack forty-foot-long parachutes and dinghies and jungle packs. My first placement was a Fleet Air Arm station just outside Edinburgh. We lived in the grounds of a convent and had to catch a little steam train to the airfield. So many days I missed the train and regularly turned up on the milk lorry, clinging desperately to the tops of the milk churns. The sudden change of life was too much, and I missed periods for exactly nine months due to shock.

But then I was sent to Machrihanish in Argyllshire which was the bad-weather station of the Fleet Air Arm.

We were sometimes visited by the chief officer in charge of all parachutes and safety equipment. He would walk around, smile at us, then leave. He was a tall, handsome man who looked terrific in his uniform. His name was Ralph Richardson and in civilian life, they said, he was an actor.

I spent eight months leaning forward against the driving rain, toiling across the bleak runways with parachutes and dinghies slung over my back to the parachute sheds. If I had been to the NAAFI and bought soap, it would foam down my legs in the blinding rain.

I felt my knees giving way. My back couldn't take any more. Then, I found that my knees did not give way and my back didn't worry, but I gradually developed big hands and wrists, for which I have been grateful in the bleak moments of my life.

Strangely enough, Gran's words of years before fell out as she had predicted. For one day, when I was twenty, I was sitting on the lavatory in a Fleet Air Arm station in Scotland, when someone pushed a yellow envelope under the door. It was a telegram to tell me that Gran was dead. She left me money enough to buy a house, which I did when the war was over. And when my husband left me later, I had a home to bring up my children in. She was right. It was my protection.

I was given a very short leave to attend her funeral. It was arranged by a cousin of hers to be done as briefly as possible. It was horrid.

I can remember being in a daze and getting on to a train in Edinburgh. The trains were full of troops, crowded on to seats, down the corridors – all over the floor, kitbags and sleeping bodies. You were spewed out of the train like a piece of battered meat.

I was driven in a white car swiftly to a cemetery, but then it was all hazy again.

The return to Scotland was in another crowded train, and when I flopped out of it, still in a trance, on to the station platform in Edinburgh, dawn was just breaking over the high rock of the castle. I realized I had left my gas mask on the train. To lose it was a serious offence and I was put on a charge before an angry captain.

Action stations

After Scotland came Ireland. I loved that. The soft everlasting rain, like a veil; the trips to whitewashed farmhouses for bacon and eggs and soda bread of such quality it was like a banquet.

Then it was my first trip overseas. I was told to pack a

kitbag with everything white, then sleep with my uniform and kitbag in a huge room not far from the Albert Hall. While I was fast asleep, a torch shone on to my face. A whisper: 'Do not speak. Just follow. Pick up kitbag and gas mask and follow.'

Through blacked-out London in a blacked-out naval lorry to a blacked-out train. In the train a WRENS officer came in the dark-blue light and whispered, 'South Africa. Boarding ship at Liverpool.'

I was pretty sick. But after a few days, managed to stagger on to the deck from our overcrowded cabin. We arrived at Port Said.

The officer in charge was charming – tall, blonde, beautiful and a bit vague. She couldn't find our papers anywhere, but she was sure she had them, somewhere. She looked all over the place. We waited. We leaned over the rail. They were fiddling about with a bit of tatty red carpet. A little group of Egyptian Army musicians played an off-key national anthem and a young King got off the boat to take refuge. We had to get off the ship – it was to travel on to South Africa without us.

So there we were, one hundred and fifty young WRENS all in virginal white, average age twenty, standing on the hot concrete in Egypt with nowhere to go. I lay down on the concrete, rested my head on the kitbag and fell asleep.

❁

The army came to sort us out and we were loaded on to a train, which took seven or eight hours slowly winding its way to Ismailia. As the train crept along the edge of the Suez Canal, men doing their ablutions waved more than their arms, and ran along by the side of the train. The bush or desert radio went into play and it was known we had arrived.

We were installed in tents on the edge of the desert. We dined on sausages, eggs and sand, oranges and sand, and encountered a lot of goodwill and big, big beetles. Our bathroom was a long pit, a plank suspended above, with holes at regular intervals. Having screamed a lot at the beetles scrambling up out of the sand, we finally fell asleep.

When we crawled out of our tents in the morning we looked up at the curve of the desert and saw a sight. As far as the eye could see were men.

The war in North Africa had been raging in the desert for two and a half years. The Eighth Army had just won a great victory at El Alamein – and I think they were all there, every one of them. They must have been up all night polishing their boots and buttons because the morning sun made them positively glitter.

Initially we were scared to leave the tents, and the Navy moved us to a brick-built camp with naval guards. Invitations came thick and so fast we had to have a rota. As regiments left the battle, they set up a camp and decided to have a bit of a do. A little dance. A bit of music. Italy had just capitulated so the place was full of Italian prisoners of war. So who better to get the party going? The artistic Italian prisoners painted beautiful invitation cards, made delicious eats from basic rations, then played wonderful music for us to dance to.

Of course, I fell madly in love. Harry was a tall South African, bronzed by the desert sun, his hair bleached gold. He was so powerful that a hug from him meant my ribs creaked, and that was how I liked it.

One great unforgettable day was a trip to the shores of Lake Timsah. Harry had hired a hawker's cart, and we were pushed down the long winding road by the lakeside. Clutching the wine and food, lots of sweet cakes and masses of roses, we sped down the road where all the Italians were camped. On either side of our cart were mesh fences about twenty feet high, with prisoners spread-eagled across them. On the ground, too, were whole armies, all pressed against the wire; singing popular songs, operatic songs, waving, laughing, and shouting heaven knows what rude things. That night in the WRENS' quarters at the brick-built fort, every single container was filled with roses.

Ah well, it was nice to dwell on a day like that, years later, when I was stuck like a sardine on a crowded Underground train going to work in some horrible shop or office, for some miserable pittance, simply so as to be able to buy the groceries for the next week.

Life in India

Our new papers had arrived. Another draft had gone to Durban, so our new destination was India. Harry moved on to Burma to join the Fourteenth Army, in time for the terrible jungle wars.

Due to the fighting in North Africa the Suez Canal had been closed, and we joined the first convoy to pass through on the way to India. Because it was expected we would be torpedoed by the Germans, we had to wear life-jackets at all times and spent many hours on deck at the ready. As we stood there, sailing silently through the Red Sea, I could see a regiment of Sikhs in their immaculate turbans, gazing towards India with longing in their eyes, as if they were willing the ship on towards their home. I was so struck by the way whole regiments and armies had rallied round in this war, coming from far and wide because they were part of the Commonwealth. They all encountered hideous scenes of war. It was such a bond. You couldn't imagine it ever melting away.

The convoy sailed through the Red Sea in complete silence. The full moon seemed to fill the sky with light. Surely the German U-boats could see us? We waited in our life-jackets. But nothing happened. I expect they had not realized the Suez Canal had been opened. We heard that by the next convoy they knew all about it, and torpedoed most of the ships in it.

Arriving in Bombay, we boarded a train to take us to Ceylon. It took a week to get us there, cooped up in our wooden carriages. Sometimes the train would stop and we ran down the track to the dining car. Stopping meant the train was soon swarming with beggars; wails of torment, and leprosy stumps waved in our faces. Not that we had money to give them, as we had to salute the captain of our 'ship' (as our camp was called) for our earnings of thirteen shillings and sixpence per week. In new money that's about seventy pence. Our wartime wages wouldn't buy a cup of coffee now.

After Colombo, I was sent to the great plains of southern India where the wind incessantly blew the red, red sand everywhere. I loved India, and used to wander around the alleyways and byways, with all their little wooden shops, in a way that shocked the expat ladies.

Our parachutes were heavy now because of the added jungle packs. They were filled with first aid, chocolate, Horlicks biscuits and other concentrated eats; not forgetting a large knife for hacking your way out of the jungle.

My first flight

The naval airfield in southern India was in full swing. Planes of all shapes and sizes were constantly arriving from the aircraft carriers to be serviced. Some were enormous, which kept us very busy in the parachute shed, checking and repacking on the long tables. We tested the dinghies in case the pilot came down in the sea, and it was important to make sure the backpacks were well packed with supplies to ensure survival in the jungle.

The officer in charge loved finding very large snakes and would walk in wearing a huge one draped all around him, holding its head in his hands. We ran screaming.

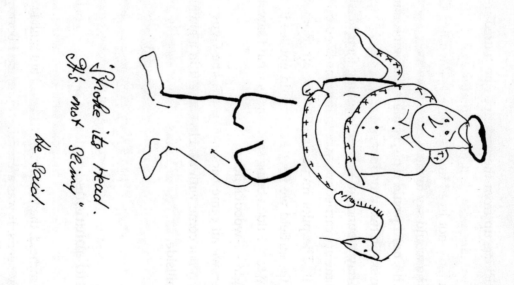

"Stroke its Head. It's not Seeing." he said.

Another young man was in charge of a Gypsy Moth, which seemed to have been left over from the First World War. He loved this tiny plane so much he seemed to regard it as his own, and his happy face could often be seen sticking up from the cockpit as he toured the airfield.

'You have not lived until you have flown in a Gypsy Moth,' he would say to me.

'Oh, no, no,' I would reply. I couldn't imagine going up into the sky in that tiny thing.

One day a bunch of sailors, laughing their heads off, picked me up, carried me over to the plane and dumped me in it. The pilot immediately took off. Round and round the airfield we flew, but I could not see it. I was clinging to the floor, being sick. That's what I saw on my first flight – a wooden floor.

When we all came back to the UK, the Gypsy Moth pilot did not come with us. He was left in a grave on a bleak hillside.

Airfield ablutions

On the airfield, the WRENS had a small hut built for their sanitary needs. It was a muddy colour, so I borrowed a bit of paint and livened up the walls with a few blue and white flowers.

The lavatory was a round hole in a piece of wood fixed over a bucket. The wall behind was cut away and covered by a plaited leaf screen which could be lifted from outside to remove the bucket. The man whose job it was had had a ticking-off for being too slow to clear the buckets, as they began to attract snakes and scorpions.

As you can imagine, every time I visited the hut, I had to check every inch of the place to see if there was a snake curled up. Outside, the man in the big white turban sat cross-legged and watched. He must have been very worried too, for as soon as you were settled, his long brown arm came shooting through the wall and snatched the bucket away.

Jungle fever

I visited Cochin and stayed on rubber plantations. Then up into the Nilgiri Hills. I got very wet in the monsoon season and developed a bad cough.

While I was rehearsing a play with the dramatic company on the camp, I started to black out with exhaustion. I went to the sick bay. I sat down in a chair, but when I tried to rise, I couldn't move. Then I saw in the mirror that all my face and the whites of my eyes were bright yellow.

'Ha, ha,' laughed the medical officer. He was an old

man – perhaps fifty, but old – and early in the morning was already well away with his gin. He had sold the beds in the sick bay, so I was laid on a native rope bed with half the rope split and broken. I dug my spine into the knot that held the frame together and waited for death.

Next to me was a girl lying on a similar wreck who moaned night and day with the tropical ulcers on her legs. I believe she lost one leg because, of course, it was 1944 and the recently discovered penicillin was hard to get hold of.

A new crowd soon arrived to take over the sick bay. They were kind and helpful, but all they could do for my jaundice was to give me doses of Epsom salts each day and nothing to eat. By now I was little more than a skeleton and well into hallucinating. So what did I see before me? Food, of course. A conveyor belt slowly passed before my eyes, loaded with Gran's food. There were her pies, her cakes, her bread and oven-bottom cakes, jam tarts, roasted chickens. They were all there and real, not at all dreamlike. Yet all I had were more Epsom salts.

When I could stand up, I took my skeleton down to meet JT by the lake. Jack Thomas was tall, dark and romantic-looking and two years younger than me. He could write boundless verse, sonnets and rhyme and talked endlessly of the plays and books he would write once the war was over.

We used to sit by the lake and watch the fireflies skimming over the water. Small girls wove long strings of jasmine and sold them on the streets. I would weave it into my hair. Oh, those perfumed nights, the flowers, the fireflies – and the open sewers, where, no doubt, I got my hepatitis.

There was one thing I can never forgive myself for. I had adopted a pi-dog who lived and slept with me constantly. I loved that little dog and I knew the hellish life of dogs roaming there. What would she do without me? I asked the new nice doctor to put her down for me when I had gone. He said he would. But that's the point. I said, *when I had gone*. I did not have the courage to be there and see it done before I left. Did he? I don't know. I can never forgive myself for my cowardice. I had a big, big cry that day.

Towards the end of my time in India, I received about twenty war-battered love letters from Harry, tied up with string, heavily censored and smelling of jungle. He had disappeared. Whole regiments were taken away overnight to fight the next phase of the dreadful war in the jungles of Burma, led by Wingate's Fourteenth Army. We had all heard of the hell they were going through, and I recall once we had the chance to lend our support.

In the middle of the night, one by one we shook each other awake – someone had said, 'They're going through.' The whole of the naval camp rushed down to the railway station. Hundreds of us stood in the moonlight on one long platform as we waited for the train. It came, chugging slowly along, and passed through the station. It was packed with British troops and from every Commonwealth country. They looked at us and we looked at them, and not a sound was heard nor a word spoken. They knew our hearts were with them and that we were just ordinary people, all caught up together in a war not of our making. So the train passed into the distance and we returned, silently, to our quarters.

The war was coming to an end and I wanted to stay in the Far East. Now Gran was gone, there was nothing for me to return to. But I was on draft and had to bring my skeleton back home.

JT and me

When I married JT in November 1945, the war was barely over and the shops were empty. For five years, nothing had been produced but armaments, and fabric shops had nothing to show but empty shelves. Luckily I had brought a silver sari back from India, which was made up into a simple but very pretty dress.

The milkman said his brother had a caravan for sale. I said, 'That's fine, I'll have it.'

The milkman said it was on Box Hill in Surrey, and his brother wanted the £300 in one-pound notes. So I went to the bank and got them.

Our house had been sold and Gran had left me £2500 to buy another, to protect me. I suppose it was quite a lot at that time, but I didn't think about it.

So it was easy to collect three hundred one-pound notes and move into a gypsy caravan on Box Hill. The air was divine and I began to feel a bit better, but food was scarce as everything was rationed.

JT got a job in a tax office, just to do until all the plays he was writing were performed and he became famous. This meant that he had to go off at the crack of dawn on his bicycle to catch a train to his office – all right in the summer, not so good in the winter.

One day early in 1946, I got up and thought for a bit. It was Saturday and JT was lying on the wooden bench that was the bed in the gypsy caravan. I said to him, 'I think I'll go out and buy a house today, are you coming?'

'No,' he said. 'I've got tummy ache.'

So I went to the station by myself. I bought a magazine

called *Homes*. It was full of houses for sale. I didn't know London at all and didn't have the slightest idea where anything was, or where to start looking. I picked up the magazine and let it drop open. Then I closed my eyes and dug at the open page with a pencil. Where had I made a mark? Talbot Road, London W2. Where was that? I wondered.

I arrived at the mainline station in London and started asking for directions, keeping the magazine open in front of me. I have no idea how I got there, but I arrived in Talbot Road, W2. The house was a large corner property. Beside it, in the street, was a square brick-built air-raid shelter.

I walked up the steps and rang the bell. A man answered the door. I showed him the magazine. 'Is this,' I said, pointing, 'this house?' He looked down at the ad.

'Yes,' he said.

'Thank you,' I said. 'I'll have it.'

And straight away I wrote him a cheque for the asking price, £1700, and handed it to him.

He said, 'Would you like to see it?' So we went inside.

It was a little bit gloomy: lavatory on the landing, a paper-peeling-off-the-wall kind of place, a few large fungi on the kitchen wall, a slight stale smell. And a family in the basement. I didn't even notice there was no bathroom. I saw the rooms were large and immediately started colouring them in my mind's eye.

Amid the gloom and cobwebs I made out two brilliant pieces of Dutch marquetry. For an extra £10 each I could have them. So I had them. A tallboy, five drawers high, and a matching drop-front bureau desk with angels and tulips climbing all over the golden wood. Later, I found two exquisite velvet hats from Paris 1890 in the bottom drawer.

We moved in. Our belongings were JT's naval toolbox and a spare carpet from my old home. I don't know what happened to all Gran's furniture. There had been a beautiful walnut suite covered with peacock-coloured velvet in the front room. What happened to that? I wonder. I expect someone bought it for about five pounds.

As we were moving in, the woman in the basement got her place condemned so she could have a council flat. The roof leaked and the fungi flourished on the kitchen wall. But we went mad with colour: red walls, white walls, yellow ceilings, a yellow front door. When we pulled up the rotten lino in the kitchen there were newspapers from 1920 and a music hall programme from 1908.

As we remodelled the house, we created a bathroom. Bob, who kept the junk shop in Ledbury Road, made his way up the stairs with a heavyweight bath on his massive back. Jim the coalman came and emptied bags of first-class coal into the cupboard under the stairs. The milkman came with his great dray horse and delivered nice, wide-top bottles. Every night at dusk, the lamplighter came with a long wand and turned the gas lamp on below our window.

One day, a great machine arrived with a ball and chain and crashed against the bomb shelter until it fell down. It was no longer required. There would be no more wars. Not after the last five years. Oh, the joy of it!

Home work

After the war, we who were young and still alive were trickling back into the world and getting married, which meant finding homes and jobs.

No job seemed to pay much money. It was never enough to manage on.

Consequently, the place was flooded with young ex-service people willing to do home work for miserable sums. Of course, businesses of every kind jumped at this need and the newspapers were full of adverts for home workers. The list was endless: threading strings of beads, sewing garments, addressing envelopes, painting lead soldiers.

❧

One job, especially, I remember doing was cutting out pictures of flowers from magazines for a firm of antique dealers in Notting Hill. They took the delicate cut-outs and placed them underneath the glass tops of dining tables to appear as place mats.

When JT had finished his day's work at the tax office and we had eaten our fill of vegetables from the Portobello Road, we would settle down with a couple of pairs of small scissors and the flower pages.

I particularly remember one lot of flowers we had to cut out – a closely packed cluster of things with tiny flowers like lilac, hydrangeas, forget-me-nots and ferns. We each had a mass of flowers to cut out, so precisely, so carefully over each tiny petal, it took us a whole week of our evenings to deliver the one bunch.

For that we were paid six old pennies each. That was the going rate, sixpence per picture per lace mat. By the time we realized how long it was going to take us we started to laugh because we were young and silly, and in the end it amused us to think how long it had taken to earn sixpence.

But we really needed the extra money, so I was always trying different things. Another small earner was painting lead soldiers. They were delivered as blank shapes, in armies. Whole regiments had to be painted complete with their horses, drums, guns, swords and all their paraphernalia. Heaven help you if it was a Scottish regiment.

Because if it *was* a Scottish regiment, you would have to paint the basic colour, then when you reached the final one, go back and paint the first line of their tartan and so on until the lines on the tartan were all complete. Considering how tiny these soldiers were, it was impossible to do them and not be covered in paint yourself and ruin everything you were wearing. For that, too, you would be paid a mere pittance.

It does mean that for ever after when you look at stuff in shops or on market stalls you think of how many hours some person has taken to paint that thing and how little they have probably been paid to do it.

Portobello culture

All around the Portobello Road was one big village. There were a few stalls on a Saturday, and it was my great treat to buy something for a shilling. A vase, antique embroidery or a piece of copper, for instance. I can still see a copper jug, filled with anemones, against a dove-grey wall. And a real baby in a vintage dress that ended up rolling out of its cradle. It was totally impractical but looked so romantic.

We bought a Victorian dining table with a beautifully inlaid top for £5. Another five pounds bought a Victorian sofa. We carried them home through the streets.

Creativity broke out in a big way. Everybody, but everybody, was writing. Writing poetry; prose; painting pictures everywhere – on the walls, on hardboard, on canvas. Plays were being performed all over the place. Little theatres started up in old shops or storerooms, even in huts at the bottoms of gardens. Plays and more plays, and the more mystical, strange and poetic they were, the more the audiences loved them.

Our friend Paul lived with his wife Lisa in a house with large white rooms. At one time one of the rooms was decorated with his paintings of the same woman with three noses, alternating with his bright-yellow pee in different-shaped glass bottles.

People were coming home from the war. The big houses were divided up into flats. Lots of people. Lots of rubbish. Dustbins in the front porch. The iron railings had gone – taken away for the war effort, they said. Dustbins everywhere, spilling out all over the patch, smelling nasty. I thought it should be neater, smell less, so I drew a design for a brown paper bag which fitted down into the dustbin, then flapped over at the top when it was full.

I sent the design to a large paper manufacturer, saying it would tidy up the rubbish.

They wrote back and said, 'No. It's a silly idea to put rubbish in bags, but here is a book about the story of our firm.' About six months later paper bags for rubbish were advertised in *The Times*. I often wondered, when I was very poor, if I would be richer had I taken out a patent. At the time, I didn't even know what they were.

Art and drama

I had just enough money now to complete my plans. They were one year at art school, one year at drama school. I went to Heatherley's School of Fine Art in Warwick Square. Every day on a 52 bus to that huge, strange house smelling of turpentine.

It suited me as it was run on easy lines. You turned up when you wanted, left when you wanted, painted whatever you wanted. I drifted from the still-life, to the life room, to the portraiture, which was my favourite. That, and flowers.

Every morning the principal, Ian McNab, came down

the great staircase wearing his long blue painting-smock to point to our failings and good bits. Other artists came to teach there too – it was a great place.

Then it was the year for acting school. Of course, I should have chosen one of the big acting schools, as having been in the forces would have been a help. But a little theatre had started up in Westbourne Grove and they were advertising for students. That suited me fine because it was just around the corner. It would be no trouble to get there and I could easily pop home for a sleep.

I still had days of exhaustion from my Indian trip, lots of chilblains and frequent colds. Sometimes when I was out I had to go down a side street and lean against a house for a while. Once when I was feeling sickly, propping myself up against a wall, a young blind man walked clumsily past me, swiping the air with his white stick. I offered to guide him but he grew loud and angry, hit the wall with his stick and shouted, 'No, no!' I expect he was one of those wounded ex-servicemen the newspapers called 'our brave lads'.

So I paid my money and went as a student to the Gateway Theatre. Through the narrow door between two shops, a long passage, then into a cosy area of chintz-covered sofas, tea bar, drinks bar. It was a dropping-in theatre where you could sit around and chat, have a drink, then go into the play if you hadn't already seen it. A real clubby club – I wish I knew one now.

People sent along boxes and boxes of old family clothes, old ballgowns, old wedding dresses, officers' uniforms from long ago. When we needed chain-mail we knitted it, then painted it silver. Poker saw to that. She was in charge of us students. Poker was really Miss Erskine with the long teeth, beautiful voice and an eternal cigarette.

The policy of the theatre was to do new plays alternately with the classics. Anybody could write a play, and they could see it performed for a fee, which would pay for the next week's classic. There was no Arts Council then. So the plays we performed were by milkmen, dustmen, diplomats, housewives, anybody. You can imagine the dialogue we had to grapple with, as well as making the costumes.

For Shakespeare, I was put on the curtain and the music. The curtain was a square of red felt, weighed down by a heavy pole, then drawn up and down with rope. For the music I had to drop the needle on to the record, which I always seemed to get one groove out. Once, I got a ticking-off from Titania.

One of our regular playwrights was a historian, who had connections with the royal family. When his play about the building of Westminster Abbey was on Queen Mary came. What an occasion it was. She was a great playgoer, and visited all the little theatres that abounded at that time.

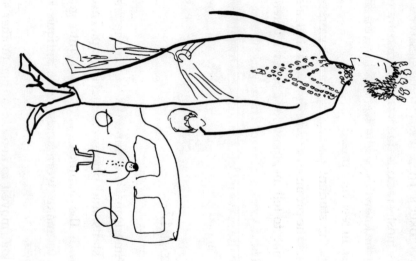

Queen Mary came in her green Rolls-Royce.

She arrived in her green Rolls-Royce, looking totally amazing in her very distinctive dress and her diamonds. With that broad diamond collar, how stunning she looked. They found an old bit of red carpet for her to walk on, and everyone had got their evening bits out of the pawnbroker's. There was a strong smell of mothballs. She was most gracious and was escorted by the playwright (she knew his mother very well) to the front row. It made you feel very proud.

When the student period ran out, I worked at the theatre for the promise of £2.50 per week. But, alas, Poker always had to tell me, 'Sorry, we haven't taken enough this week.'

Winter 1947

Some Americans had started to visit the Portobello market stalls, and prices were going up. The air was filled with the hammering of nails into good new wood, to make wormholes. The antique industry flourished.

Lisa had moved to another of her mother's houses, while Paul had found religion and had gone to Cornwall to contemplate. He moved off in his little box of a car,

I think it was an Austin 8. The doors were broken and tied up with string; the weather was bitterly cold so he had a little oil stove standing on the floor of the car. Before he left, he gave me a painting left over from his exhibition. A lady with three noses, playing a piano.

Lisa's new home was her childhood home, a large corner house, where the high fence curved around the side and a long, long flight of steps led up to the back door. Those steps were the scenes of dramas. Once, a young writer whose book had hit the headlines stayed there with a girl. But he had a wife, and her father arrived and whipped him with a horsewhip all the way down the steps. It was in all the papers. When things happened in that area, it was news.

Another time, a rejected lover stood at the top of the steps and threw the large collection of milk bottles by the back door crashing down to the bottom, one by one.

The winter of 1947 was bitterly cold. The snow settled and lasted for weeks on the ground. It held hard on to the pavements and made slippery, rock-hard mountains. London was frozen solid. The great tall houses of Talbot Road were shrouded in a dark-grey icy mist, which hung in the air.

Our Betty

Once, returning from a night out, we climbed up the steps and entered the long, dark hallway. From somewhere in the darkness, something else fell through the doorway with us. It was a cat.

When we saw it in the light we fell about with pity. Its black fur had coagulated into wet lumps, showing its sad body. Its nose and cheeks were bloody as if hit by a stone

Barabbas.
my first cat.

or a brick, and it was desperately hungry. In such a state, in fact, that it would have to be put down so as to put it out of its misery. We shut it in a room with some food, planning to take it to the vet the next day.

Of course, neither of us had courage enough to do that, so we just kept on feeding it. This caused all his wretched fur to drop out and a magnificent new coat to grow, with a great ruff.

That was the beginning of my love for cats. How could I not have noticed before how beautiful they were? My only other contact had been the kitten being sick in my knickers many years before. I was brought up to think they were vermin, like Mrs Thompson did, with her gun at the ready in case they walked on her lawn.

'As he is a thief who has been reprieved, he shall be called Barabbas,' said JT, who had a way with words.

Soon afterwards, a woman knocked on the door with something in her hand, like a tennis ball. She said a crowd of boys were tossing it to each other in the street for fun. It was a very tiny cat curled up like a fist, taut with fear. She never grew big, and had a little two-colour face. We named her Yorick.

Our Betty

Yorick

Exercises on breathing

Things changed a bit. One day the milkman came with tears running down his cheeks, saying that the dairy had bought new milk floats and his beloved Dolly was going to the knacker's yard with all the rest of those great, strong horses.

89

I worked hard at the theatre, did everything, swept the stage, knitted the chain-mail, hauled the red felt curtain up and down, sometimes bringing the heavy pole crashing down on to the stage.

But then there were lessons and students' show nights and that lovely contact with the audience, even if there were only a few out there. I played parts in the new plays, but in the classics I was only in crowd scenes. I was given a part in a Greek tragedy, but when people fell about laughing was quickly dropped into the bunch of captured slaves. When I bent over in subservience once, rain dripped from the leaky roof down my back. Poker made us Grecian garments from mutton cloth she had managed to find.

The leads in the Greek and Shakespearean plays were played by old actors who had had great experience on the boards. Some had been names. Some had nearly been names. Or had worked with names.

Their acting was often of an earlier time and done with great gusto. It was the acting of the endless tours they had done all over the British Isles, sometimes only staying one night, carrying everything in a skip, sleeping anywhere, always on a train going somewhere else, working for a pittance. Always hoping for a big theatre booking, hoping to be noticed, to get something in the West End and have work for months.

Voices throbbed; gestures came from the heart, literally. I have known the word 'go' take minutes, frozen in the air while the actor placed his index finger on his heart, then slowly pointed to the wings.

So we learned timing with our audiences. Mine was based on the teachings of Mrs Sellick, who had taught me more than I had realized at the time. Now came exercises for the voice. For this I went to a lady making me 'Oh' and 'Ah' up and down the scale, and a lot more. Her father, Professor J. Richardson, had been in charge of voice production at the Guildhall School of Music, and her teachings were based on his little book – price, fourpence – entitled *Exercises on Breathing*: tone, formation, articulation, modulation, inflection, point- and word-painting.

I worked at these exercises for a long time, but nothing seemed to happen. However, later in my life, in big theatres, I found my voice shot right to the back row of the gallery. So it works. My little fourpenny book, now yellow with age, could be very useful today for many a television actor who gets a job on the stage.

London life

Everyday we visited the Portobello Road. No fridge, no food storage, just a trip down there each day to buy, to cook, then to eat. It was glorious. The stalls were heaped with everything, although it was still rationed, of course. When we were lucky, we found a bit of meat, one stale egg, a scrap of dry cheese. But there was always plenty of fish. Government leaflets told you how good carrots were, and encouraged you to eat whale meat. I bought some and it was disgusting – like solid cod liver oil. But vegetables, vegetables of every kind – some I had never seen before. The place was a riot of colour. I began to feel better, put on some weight. The colds and chilblains went away.

JT was still writing plays and books. I used to go off to perform at the theatre, then come rushing home to hear him read what he had written that evening. We dreamed dreams.

But alas, the pile of scripts grew and grew, each one with its rejection slips. With each rejection slip JT's moods grew darker, until at times they could be very dark indeed. So a lot of the time he was not much fun to live with, but he could still be very witty and good company.

❧

A man came to the door. He was a pleasant, friendly man. So sorry, he said, but as I had not paid any rates, would I please go to the Magistrates' Court on such and such a date?

What rates? I hadn't seen any rates. What were rates? If they had lain on the doormat in the shadowy hall somebody must have picked them up before I saw them.

Anyway, that was no excuse, so I had to go to the court and stand between two huge policemen and stammer out any kind of apology as to why the rates had not been paid, even though I didn't know why. Of course, they had to be paid, and so I now started my trips around Knightsbridge and Regent Street, selling off treasures: bits of silver, Japanese ceramics, embroidered things from India.

JT trailed down the road with a heavy bag of his favourite records.

'One day,' he said, 'there'll be a whole opera, a whole symphony, on one thing, not eight heavy records.'

It was so humiliating and such a disgrace to my small provincial mind to be hauled up in a court for debt, and have to stand there between two big policemen. But that was only the beginning. After that, it happened every time the rates were due. Do you know, I got used to it!

It ceased to bother me. The man became quite friendly. We greeted each other when he came. 'It's the same again,' he would say.

'OK, that's all right.' Sell some more stuff and pay up. It was all part of life.

Apart from Lisa, another good friend at that time was Rita Webb, one of the very colourful characters in the area. She lived nearby and I would sit in her kitchen for hours on end, where she would tell me tales of her remarkable life. She was always trying to get parts in television. And she succeeded; she was a great character with a huge warm heart.

'Hello,' she would say. 'Hello, this is not just the best actress in London ringing you, not the best actress in the country, but in the *whole world*.'

It worked, and she worked. Her beloved Geoff would sit happily by, playing his banjo. He was a very good musician. He taught music and accompanied singers.

Many times Ewan MacColl came and sat in the kitchen with us. He sang and sang with his hand cupped to his ear, Geoff played, and Rita fed them sandwiches. Sometimes she would whisper, 'Be quiet tonight, Diana Dors is asleep upstairs, she has to be up at six because she's filming.'

Another time she had another friend sleeping on the

put-me-up. 'She's come from the north,' said Rita. 'She tours around with plays but she wants to find a theatre in London, so she's staying here to look. She's called Joan Littlewood.'

Portobello was just like a village then. Regularly I jumped out of bed at five in the morning and pressed my nose against the window when the horses and carriages of the Royal Artillery swept through the streets on a practice trot. What a sight to see from the upstairs window, the glorious long backs of those horses, their hoofs clattering through the city streets. What a lovely place it was to live. Even though the fungi still grew on the kitchen wall.

Into Epping Forest

Because I had been robbed of family in my childhood, I wanted to have a family of my own more than anything in the world. In 1950 I had a daughter, Sarah, and in 1954, a son, Robert. To have two children was a dream come true.

At that point I started to feel a desire to have a garden for us to play in, so I decided to sell the house in Talbot Road.

Alas, this was easier said than done. Unlike I had, people did not arrive on the doorstep and just ask to buy it, but actually wanted to look at it first. Of course, when they looked they saw the huge bend in the outer wall, the condemned basement and the roof with holes in it. So they didn't buy.

Perhaps they should have done, for later it was worth more than a million pounds. Even now, in a new millennium, I have nightmares about that roof.

Eventually, a man came along, stood by the wall I'd painted a beautiful soft red and seemed fascinated by it. He came back, and again, and stood at the end of the red wall. He had come over with the Polish army to fight in the war and had an amazing Polish name. He wanted to buy it. The basement didn't bother him; he collected prints, so it would be great for storage.

But because of the condition of the house, he couldn't get a mortgage. We had to come to some arrangement. So I sold it to him for the price I had paid, £1700. Mr Ifeorski Leinkerwitz had only £300. This three hundred he could give me, the rest he promised to send me in instalments of £10 a month. I accepted it – and little did I know then how much I would come to rely on that £10 a month.

Now to find a place with a garden. It had to be simple, easy to find. We took the Central Line, aimed towards

Epping Forest. There was a house for sale at the top of a hill, backing on to part of the forest. The garden was south-facing and wild, running into trees.

I could put down my £300 and take out a mortgage, so I did. On moving day, our Victorian pieces went in a van and we went by Underground. JT carried baby Robert. Little Sarah walked, and I carried Yorick in a pillowcase tied around her chin. Our small group climbed up the hill, and thank goodness there was a seat halfway up. We had a bit of a rest, then walked the last bit. It is a very steep hill.

The garden was a magic place for people, or cats. Wild, long grass hedges shot up to what looked like 30 feet high. Wisteria and lilac grew rampant. Hedges of mock orange grew on either side of the front path, leaning over towards each other, making a tunnel. At blossom time, scented water dripped when it rained. A laburnum tree hung over the front gate and roses climbed crazily up the front and back of the house. Bluebells came with the spring, and a large toad lived in the cellar. He was not alone down there, for in a crack where a door had been ran a little stream where newts played; when the snow melted in the forest, the water gushed.

Our house was half of a very large house divided into two. Our neighbours on the other side had a huge garden running into the forest, and an old stable where goats and chickens lived. Their garden produced apples, pears and cherries.

Our house was the side that had not had any work done so far that century. So, guess what? The roof leaked.

We arrive in the Suburbs.

The water pipes were made of lead and draped in large loops around the walls of the back rooms. Melted, no doubt, in the long hot summers of long ago.

The only heating came from the Victorian fireplaces. A walk in the forest gave plenty of wood to throw on, which seemed, in the beginning, a romantic thing to do. But I soon changed my mind.

Feeling all rural, I was having a cup of tea and throwing wood on the fire. Within minutes, as the heat crept into the wood, the insects began to run out. Every size and shape of creepy-crawly running for their lives.

'Oh! Oh!' Screams and shudders.

So in winter Jack Frost decorated the windows during the night, and if you should leave a cup of water on the flagged floor, by morning it was solid ice. When you spoke in the living room, an icy mist appeared before your face. When the wind blew, you must crouch in front of the fire until your front bits were burning red blotches, but hold a hankie out and it would shiver like a ship in full sail.

Getting up in the morning could be a terrible experience. Just a shuddering body under inadequate blankets and a nose sticking up into the air like an icicle.

Of course, summer was lovely in the south-facing

garden. You could lie in the long grass with the daisies and watch every kind of bird that passed in and out of the forest.

The pity of war

Exploring the area, we walked under the chestnut trees along the High Road to Woodford Green, where the cows roam.

The High Road runs for miles and miles until it reaches Epping. You can look down it and see for miles. It looks pretty with the trees, an old church, a village green where people play cricket, and a large and ancient school.

On we walked into Woodford Green to the shops and to the doorway of the chemist's, where a woman stood. She was growing old, but every single day since the war ended she stood in the doorway, looking down the High Road. Waiting for her son to come home.

She must have been there for nearly ten years by the time I met her, and I imagine she was there until she died. Every day she powdered her face, and as the years passed her powder grew thicker and more careless. And that is how I see the war. Not the speeches and the big noisy battles, the leaders clutching at their hearts and declaring their sympathy for the loss of young lives. No, it's the empty roads and the empty rooms where people stand and wait but no one comes. It's the silence that goes on after the shouting has died down.

There is a statue on the High Road of someone whose words we couldn't have managed without during the war. It is the local MP, Winston Churchill.

Curtain-twitching

Sarah started school when Robert was just a few months old. I pushed him in his pram up and down the orderly tree-lined roads of this mind-numbingly prissy, dull suburb. Endlessly.

I felt as if I had been hit over the head with a railway sleeper to deaden the senses, and there was another me floating about somewhere outside my body but I couldn't find it.

On past interminable roads of unreal houses. They seemed like cardboard cut-outs, on a film set, waiting for the actors to arrive, for there were no people about. The roads were empty, dead.

The gardens immaculate and tidy, stocked with flowers so perfect they looked as if they were plucked from the catalogue. The lawns, green stretches where a daisy would not dare to raise its head. Big expensive cars stood next to the garden gnomes.

What had I done? Oh, the deadness of it all. Oh, the silence. Nobody here was writing poetry and painting pictures. I'm sure they were somewhere, but not here.

For Robert's first birthday, I bought a whippy rotary garden spray, and on hot days we ran through it, screaming. It was moments like those that made the move worthwhile. But on the whole I still felt that my life supply had been turned off.

Anyway, we settled in, determined to be part of the scene. We thought it a good idea to join the local community centre – that's what you did in places like this. I joined the pottery class. I came back and told JT all about it. So he joined.

Very, very soon he was having to pop round there to take his pot out of the oven. Or, as I found out later, maybe put his pot into the oven.

Things grew a bit strange, until one day he went down with pneumonia and was whisked off to hospital. Well, I had never been that far out before and had to walk down a long road, way beyond Epping, so I was very late arriving for the visit. Another lady potter from the class had arrived first, and was sitting fondly by his sickbed.

I ran down the road from the hospital. It was one of those January days that never get light, just a black sullen sky, sheeting down with rain. Rain or tears, no one would have been able to tell.

On the day he was expected home, the children decorated the front porch with Christmas trimmings and the neighbour left a bowl of eggs sitting on the front step. Well, we waited and waited, but he didn't arrive back from the lady potter's house until her husband came home.

Then he arranged to leave.

Well, what can you say about broken marriages and divorce? The worst pain seems to last for about eighteen months. That's when you walk about the streets crying out loud and not caring if people see you. That's when you become a social outcast. That's when all the neighbours cross the road when they see you coming, in case they have to say hello.

And all the lace curtains were flapping. I was in the wrong place for such a thing to happen. Believe me, if anything rotten is going to happen to you, make sure it's not in a mealy miserable suburb, but in a place where life is lived.

So here I was, in a dark and crumbling house with a two- and a six-year-old, surrounded by all this negativity. And no money. In the mid-1950s, there was no help for a lone parent – in fact it was regarded more as a disgrace. I was awarded alimony of £5 per week and thirty shillings for each child.

But here stepped in my dear friends at the Inland Revenue. They retained a sum of money, and I had to beg on a printed form to get some of it back. I was left with £23 a month. At that time there was no child allowance for the first child, just eight shillings (40 new pence) for the second. I'm telling you all this because my eyes pop out when I read of the going rates today and the help that is given on demand.

Not that I was the worst off. Some of the women I met in my search for schools were harder hit when their husbands just disappeared without trace – and no money at all, and no house. They had to take jobs as skivvies in private houses or hotels just to put a roof over their heads. My roof was over my head even if it was leaking, and even if my interest in the house was slender.

And what was it that saved my bacon? Well, of course, the £10 each month from Mr Ifeorski Leinkerwitz. If he had stopped, I would have had to stop. But he didn't stop. Thank you from way back, Mr Stanislas Ziegmunt Ifeorski Leinkerwitz, you were a man of honour.

Getting on, getting by

We dressed from jumble sales. Jumble sales became part of life for us. I made a coat out of an old pale-yellow velvet curtain. An old lady up the road said it looked good. I couldn't afford stockings. I bought loads of old china for a few pence, brought it home and hurled it piece by piece against the wall. I did that instinctively, but now I realize it did me a lot of good. At the time we just do things, though, don't we?

Never mind jumble sale clothes, the most important thing was food. I bought a Mouli, and every day squeezed every kind of vegetable through it. Thick, thick soup, handfuls of parsley on top, grated cheese – yummy yummy. For a treat, a piece of brisket cooked in a pot in the iron oven with more and more vegetables. Oatcakes, chocolate cakes, and chestnuts roasted on the open fire.

Cats and more cats started to drift towards me. Some of them I kept, some of them were strays. But how could I feed them on my meagre money? Luckily, down the road was a truly wonderful fishmonger, who for as little as sixpence gave me a bag of fish pieces of gigantic proportions. Bless you, David, for all your fish favours. He's still there with his freshly caught fish, and now he has a real wood-fired smokery.

People began to dump strays on me. Some I fostered for the RSPCA. There was a cats' home nearby that was always running out of money, so I started to have cat jumble sales in my garden.

Music, flags in the trees, homemade cakes. I had loads of offers of help. The ladies wanting to help with the sorting taught me a lot about ladies who help with charity dos. Diving into heaps of unsorted stuff, then rolling up the prime pickings into a ball, just making sure you never saw what goodies they had. Not just clothes, either – they had an eye for antique clocks that only needed a spot of Brasso, or an old violin that could easily have been a Stradivarius.

Auntie Laura

But I was stuck here and unable to move in any direction. As I was still such an outcast, my longings turned towards acting. All the lovely warm feelings I had had from the church halls when I was a child and the audiences at the Gateway and the little theatres made me eager for one more chance.

My relief, this time, came from a postcard in the newsagent's window. It said someone needed a place to stay for herself and small child, in exchange for some help. No sooner had I answered the message than there was a knock at the door. I opened it, and there she stood, the picture of a woman you could just hand a child to and know he or she would be cared for.

She was Auntie Laura from the first moment. She had six children but just brought the little one with her. That child was the same age as Robert so they played together. Auntie Laura had left her husband to be with Bill. So it suited her well to live in the same road as him. And it suited me well because now I could look for work. So we filled each other's needs and no money passed between us, ever. We only exchanged help to each other.

Auntie came to the door.

Odd jobs

I started writing off for auditions and took the actors'
magazine, *The Stage*. But finding work that would bring
in some money was quite a problem because I couldn't
do anything.

My first job was down the road in a plastic-bag factory. It was a rather curious arrangement. A crowd of women sat around a large table and in front of each was a pile of plastic bags. This was the drill: put your arms into the top bag, lift it up and look for holes. If it had a hole, put it down left. No hole, put it down right. Then the same with the rest, then start again with a new pile. All day, all day, just that – from nine to five, looking at plastic bags.

They were a friendly lot, all very nice women. Each day started with chat, which as the day wore on got more and more lively, until by teatime it was positively filthy.

So by the afternoon we were rocking and screeched into the plastic bags, looking for holes and finding the most obscene stories to tell, all trying to outdo each other talking dirty. We ended the day like a bunch of drunken sailors, then pulled ourselves together and walked out into the street looking like women who had earned their bread that day looking for holes in plastic bags.

One day, as I passed by the post office I saw a notice in the window for a one-delivery postman. So I went in and asked, 'Could it be a postwoman?'

They thought it over very seriously and said yes. Well,

I did it for quite a long time until my legs could hardly move.

They kitted me out in a uniform and I had to carry a heavy bag up and down concrete stairs in a horrible block of flats. I was not a success at this job. I should have been up at 4 a.m., but the post office was just over the road and many times the postmaster came banging on my window shouting for me to 'get out of that bloody bed and get them letters sorted'.

There was a postal delivery on Christmas Day and I had to be brought home in a wheelbarrow because I could not walk another step. But there was Christmas dinner to cook. I had read somewhere a rather good recipe for rum punch. It was rather strong, but buoyed me up enough to get on with the cooking.

JT was coming to dinner. He arrived on a tandem with the lady potter. He came to see his children and she went to see hers. My Christmas present was a lavatory seat – the old one had wormholes. Another glass of punch was called for. Considering these were my first drinks of the year, it was amazing they lasted until the sprouts were cooking.

Then darkness descended upon me and I spent Christmas dinner under the table. It was a battered old table draped in red gingham. And that's how I saw several Christmases. From the underside of the table, my two legs sticking out beyond a fringe of red gingham. Family above, eating a thin chicken.

Christmas Day

Giving it a try

I continued with the pleas for auditions. The battered little photographs were sometimes returned, many not even saying who they were from. What a blessing it was for me to find the Unity Theatre at that time. I was still raw, still in the depths of despair because of the collapse of my marriage, still an outcast in my own street.

Friends had faded away into the shadows, and if I sought comfort in going to church the pious congregation only drew closer together, just giving me the odd sideways glance. It was the same in pubs. If I went in for a friendly little drink, I would only be left isolated by sidelong glances, until the sherry choked in my gullet.

But then I joined the Unity Theatre. I put on some old boots and a feather boa and sang Nellie Wallace songs, and they all roared from the balcony. It was then I found the advice in the fourpenny booklet had worked on my voice, and the audience really could hear me in the back row. The people there were lovely, friendly, relaxed and with a wider view of life than in the prissy suburb where I lived.

Now and then there was a play such as the very good production of *Death of a Salesman* by Arthur Miller in which I played Mrs Loman, and George Bernard Shaw's *Heartbreak House.*

There was a job going at the local delicatessen and I gave it a try. But I was utterly bewildered by the hundreds of sausages and cheeses and other foods I had never come across before. I stood there, knowing I had a lost look on my face. The other assistants had a bit of a snigger at me. But I was the new girl, and got all the rotten jobs, so I had to learn quick. Up and down, up and down the cellar steps, hauling up the great wheels of maggot-infested cheeses and being shouted at by the customers: 'You've served her before me. It's me first. Me, me, me.' I hadn't noticed.

Some customers came in the morning in one outfit and in a different one in the afternoon. Little white gloves and shopping baskets, and big cars by the pavement outside. Their exotic holidays had given them the fondness for this kind of food. I was paid £5, less than a pound a day for a five-and-a-half-day week, but I learned to serve in a shop.

I continued with more appeals for auditions, or to agents to put me on their books, but all to the chorus of 'No, no, no. Go away.'

In order to be ready for any theatrical job, I decided to be a shop demonstrator, which meant I could leave at one day's notice when the big moment came. So now I was one of those tiresome people standing there spouting to the passing throng about the advantages of this bread or biscuit, this flower vase, this silk scarf, this jam or marmalade, this cooking pot, this pair of scissors, this food mixer. This absolutely anything. It was always the best, and I found myself at one time or another in every possible kind of shop and exhibition.

Learning to fly

I had read in *The Stage* about an American called Charles Marowitz coming over here to start a company based on the acting discipline known as 'the Method'. I went along, and I became one of his little band. There weren't very many of us. I think it was about eight.

The British Drama League allowed us to use their tiny theatre in Fitzroy Square in central London, and there we started improvisations most nights of the week. In the day we must work, for Charles paid us no money. Anyway, work hard we did in the evenings too, improvising through one story after another and revealing more and more of ourselves until we felt like gutted fish laid out on a slab.

He called it 'the Hi Style' and that's what it was, because we became high. We were so tuned in to each other that we could anticipate which word might come next. Sometimes, after an improvisation, Charles would show us a short play that was the improv only he had written it before we had done it. Strange things floated in when we were in this receptive frame of mind.

Once, hit by a sudden crisis when a partner could not speak, I just dried up too. This was at a time when only a few people came to watch. Charles had opened it up to an audience when we had been improvising for over a year. For, you see, we had all the time in the world – we were a permanent company in the Russian manner (Charles had come from Russia to New York) – and would work together for the rest of our lives.

Anyway, one particular night, the planned improv dried up completely, so we had to shoot out our antennae from the tops of our heads and into infinite space. The idea that beamed in was that the bomb had fallen. So here we were, the only two people left, in complete devastation, and we must make our way to an underground retreat until the mess had cleared and we could once again create England's green and pleasant land. We went off singing 'Jerusalem'. A week later, it was reported in the *Daily Telegraph* that a party of people had done just that. And their names were the ones we had used.

It's all there, isn't it? It's all singing around our heads, but I think we get too busy to pick it up. If only we could let ourselves float.

It was during the nightly visits to the Drama League that my divorce came through. It was the first one of the day at the law courts in the Strand, so by 10.45 it was over. JT asked if I wanted a coffee, so we went over the road and had one. Then, there was a stunning new painting at the National Gallery, so we went to see it; in the afternoon, a Jacques Tati film, *Mon Uncle*, where we laughed ourselves silly. Afterwards, JT accompanied me to the door for the next rehearsal.

He said, 'Apart from its rather unusual beginning, it's been a lovely day.' As I said, JT had a way with words.

So Charles had opened the improvisations to an audience. I had stopped my eternal requests for auditions because we must stay as a permanent company. A few people came and sat in the audience. Then a lot of people came. The university was just beyond at Tottenham Court Road, and a lot came from there. Then whole crowds of them came. There were not enough seats, and there was much hammering at the door. Charles put a large enamel bowl by the door to collect offerings. Some people dropped five-pound notes in there, but we did not see any money.

And the Hi Style flourished. Once we went to Dublin on the promise of £7, but the theatre went bankrupt. So we were in the pawnshop with everything we had. Letters were sent home. 'Send me a pound,' we wrote, 'we are starving.' JT sent a pound, and we had soup and sweet buns from the delicious-smelling bakery. The children were with me. Robert was now six years old. Sarah, ten. We loved Dublin. The people were so kind to us, and we spent the days on those lovely beaches and the nights doing improvisations, when amazing things happened. Words came out of their own accord.

The Hi Style continued until our fifth year together. Then, one night, I just turned up as usual. I said, 'Charles is late. It's unusual for him.' 'He's dumped us and gone to work with Peter Brook at the RSC,' I was told. He didn't even say goodbye.

I took *The Stage* again and started to call on agents. I was snubbed and treated most rudely. One visit was outstanding. It was to a woman agent whose name I fortunately can't remember.

'Why?' she screamed at me as she pointed to the door. Why had I the cheek to approach her office? 'Get out. Get out!' Who was I? Nobody.

'Out, out, get out of my sight. Don't waste my time!'

I stumbled down her little dark stairs and into the street, so numbed that it was a year before I tried anyone again.

School

Back in the suburbs, the children were growing up amidst all those shoulder-jerking, self-satisfied curtain-twitchers. How to get them out of it? I looked for schools. The British Legion helped me because of my war service, so through them I applied for the greatest school I could find. It was in Witley, near Godalming, an ancient foundation moved from London to a glorious situation in Surrey. In another stroke of luck, we were accepted.

Sarah was very good at interviews. She wore the little sailor suit from Marks & Spencer that JT had bought her as a farewell present. She paved the way for Robert to go there when he too was ten.

The wonderful Educational Committee of Essex backed us to the hilt. Looking back, I realize times have changed and I'm sure you couldn't do it now. But fate must have dictated why we had to leave all the excitement of the Portobello Road. Thank you, Essex.

Equus

Sometimes our wishes can come true. When Robert was twelve and on holiday from school, I thought he should see Peter Shaffer's *Equus*, which was running at the Old Vic Theatre. It was a highly thought-of play and I felt he had to see it for his education to be complete.

We scrambled our pennies together, digging into pots and jars and down backs of sofas until we had enough. Typical of my careless ways, when we were standing in the theatre we realized we were a little bit short of the price of the tickets. Not quite enough pennies had been found. We implored the man in the box office to adjust the price a bit, but were disdainfully dismissed.

The crowded foyer was beginning to thin out, which meant the play would soon begin. This is the way with London audiences – they always pile in at the last moment. I was aware Orson Welles had been standing at the side and now he had gone.

Robert spoke fiercely to me: 'You stand there. I'll stand here. Something will happen.'

We stood in deep concentration, and within minutes he had bent down and found a few postage stamps, just enough to complete the price of our seats. With a scowl, old miseryguts in the box office gave us our tickets. You see, our dreams may not *always* come true, but it's worth a try.

It's expensive to be poor

By the end of the 1960s, life had developed a definite pattern. The summers were spent by the sea at the Butlin's camp, doing plays with the Forbes Russell Repertory Company. For many of the campers it was their only chance to see theatre, and they loved it. I believe, for many, it was the reason they chose Butlin's for their holiday.

For the growing children, and for me, Butlin's was a godsend. All those weeks of sea air and sand set us up for the long winter months. We came back glowing. I saw myself reduced within weeks to the same weary state, though, and felt perhaps I should live by the sea. But we didn't. The children went back to school, and I to the shops to work, or to offices.

If anything, the offices were worse than the shops because I couldn't do anything there except filing, and that filled me with screaming boredom.

Often I would look at the clock thinking I must have been there for hours, and it was only ten past nine. In one office, a man went mad with anger because someone had put their coat on his peg. He had simply put his coat on the same peg for forty years. I felt trapped.

At least there was more entertainment in the shops, although the hours were endless and some of the super-visors were dragons. Once, in Hamleys, I saw a friend walk into the shop, top to toe in very expensive black leather. She looked so rich I couldn't bear it. She must not see me. I ducked under the counter and begged them to let me know when she had gone.

I tried being a telephonist, and had to go on a course to learn how to plug in all over the country. I was so tired because of doing the improvising most nights that I could hardly keep awake. So I developed a state of semi-coma, in which I could sleep but still hear when the questions were aimed at me.

When the instructor announced who had passed, she added, when she got to my name, 'Passed, in spite of being sound asleep all the time'! I was amazed she had noticed.

So I became a GPO telephonist. Alas, it didn't last long. I did all the wrong things – I just didn't go the right way about connecting people who wanted to speak to

Birmingham or Edinburgh. The final blow came when I went to get a new pen to twiddle the dial with and they simply handed me an 'international pen', because my hair was black in those days and they'd decided I was Italian. But they were grateful to grab at any excuse, and I was invited to go home, never to return.

I went home, and it was snowing. Robert was sitting there crying, with a row of buckets and bowls catching the leaks from the roof. So when the electricity company paid me £400 for a piece of land at the bottom of the garden to put in an electric generator, I finally had the roof repaired. At least, I thought it had been repaired. The builder went busily up and down the ladder with a bucket of stuff, but of course he was a cowboy and I never really got rid of the leak. I discovered that it is very expensive to be poor.

Seaside days

But the summers by the sea continued to be lovely. The three of us packed ourselves into a caravan, and we always bought bikes for a few shillings and rode around the countryside during the day.

I have always loved the seaside. When I was little, we

went frequently to Bridlington. What long happy hours I spent on the beach there.

Miles of glorious sand, with so many happenings: sand artist performers with their frilly neck-pieces holding little competitions for us kids, Punch and Judy, and of course, the eternal sea creeping up to flood our sandcastles. After the beach came the ice-cream in the Floral Hall. Great big knickerbocker glories, and a trio of ladies playing popular music who always dressed in long black satin dresses with hanging sleeves lined with white. I thought they were penguins. One day on our way to the ice-cream parlour a seer stood in our path, lifted his pale blue eyes and his arms to the sky saying, 'Long may you live, lady, your life is required.'

But in the 1960s it was a caravan in a field, with sheep or cows. We had cow friends at Skegness. Their faces looked at us through a sea of sweet smelling cow parsley until early one morning, rough men came with sticks and loud voices. Then, later in the day, we saw our friends hanging, halved and still steaming.

Some years later, the *Sunday Times* printed a supplement called *What We Do to Animals*. This brilliant and terrifying piece showed in graphic detail, including close-ups in slaughter houses, exactly what we, in this animal-loving country, do to most animals raised for food. It had such an effect on me that I have never eaten meat since.

The tide turns

So summers turn to winters, and Butlin's to toy shops for Christmas. Very often I felt mean, selling a box of nothings done up in bright colours to someone eager to please their children. The ones that hurt me most were the hard-working, loving parents, who had had to take out loans to buy the toys their children asked for. As I took the money from them I could feel the calluses on their hands. So they would be doing some rotten job for months to pay off the debt for that box of bits that would be broken long before they were paid for.

And I was part of that chain, doing what I did just to feed my family, when really I should have cried out, 'Don't buy it, it's rubbish.'

But towards the end of the 1960s, it was mostly Hamleys at Christmas – the old original shop, which was narrow and packed. The buying and selling was frantic. Many a mother, father, grandma, uncle, aunt or god-mother assured me they had to choose carefully because the child was exceptionally bright. As the day wore on, the dust would rise from the old floors. People became insistent that you served them next – one solid mass, a sea of popping mouths.

One afternoon just before Christmas, I was serving somebody with a little toy car when I glanced up across the upturned faces and saw another shop assistant holding a phone high into the air. Her finger pointed first to it, then to me. I dived into the crowd and pressed my way through to the phone.

A voice said, 'Have you heard that a young film director is planning to make his first fully improvised feature film?' He had found the young people he needed, but wanted an older woman who could improvise to play the mother. He was seeing people at Spotlight. His name was Mike Leigh.

So the magic happened.

I went to Spotlight and met Mike. He said I could come along to his audition, to be held in a church hall in north London. The improvisation was this: we were waiting to be picked up to go to a hospital outpatients' department.

We were dispersed around the hall, took up our own corner, which was our home, and waited in our own way. If you fell asleep, well, that's what you did. But whatever you did, there was always this pair of shining dark eyes peering over chairs, under chairs, popping up over drawers and cupboards. Mike was everywhere, missing nothing. We improvised for four hours, then were told to 'come out of character'.

I was thrilled when I got that job. Now I had to improvise so as to find the character. This took weeks and weeks, going mostly to another rehearsal room to be this difficult old mother. Her main aim was never to get out of bed, so I spent all those weeks in bed, knitting endlessly and seamlessly, insisting on taking my teeth out and twiddling with a little radio. She was like a butterfly, alighting on various radio stations, stopping and starting, doing and undoing the knitting.

In another room, more improvisations were going on with someone who was to visit me. We never met until much later, when she came into my room.

She was a mentally deficient girl, and she sat by my bedside, communicating in her own way. Me mumbling, fiddling with the radio and knitting, though she sat so close to me. I totally believed that her mind was impaired, so great was her acting. She had become that girl.

I think this is one of the most difficult things to do. To attempt a part like this can just be embarrassing. I cringe when I think of Forrest Gump. I marvel when I remember Leonardo DiCaprio in *What's Eating Gilbert Grape?*. But Sarah Stephenson did it.

Anyway, the time came when we all knew who we were and filming could start. My bits were done in a flat in Kentish Town. I sat in the bed. The theme of the room was frogs and they were everywhere – glass ones, china ones, wooden ones, all sorts. The traffic thundered down the street. It thundered so hard the camera couldn't take it, so filming couldn't start before 10.30 or 11 p.m. Improvising throughout the night until about seven next morning was strange and exciting. By 3 a.m. it all felt very real and I loved it so much I hoped it would go on for ever.

I went home in the morning when all the early workers were coming in, when their heads were already down with the cares of the day and mine was floating around with happiness like a loose balloon. I was still deep in the improvisations, sitting on the Central Line with a silly smile on my face.

I had found a new beginning. The contract was for three days at £10 a day, and I was in heaven. Fancy being so happy and getting paid for it! What a life.

Of course, it couldn't last for ever, and soon it was over. I was back to the old routine – going to work, and decorating the old house.

Mike's film came out in 1971. It was called *Bleak Moments*. It was a huge success and won him prizes. The headlines were an inch high.

A garden of delights

Although our house was in need of repair, the garden was magic. The pear tree was very old and every year produced a heap of pears that were rock-hard and impossible to use. But if I left them in my iron oven for two days, they came out the colour of rubies with a rich, strong, intense flavour. They were absolutely delicious.

The neighbours always kept a few goats and some chickens in the old stables on the edge of the forest. We ate the goat's milk yoghurt with a trickle of honey.

Another thing that came from the neighbours' huge garden was the harvest of fallen apples. They had cherry and apple trees, along with strange items like a bowl of old taps and pews from a bombed-out church.

The fruit trees gave forth plenty. The cherries were a sight to behold and the apples pushed each other off the bough, but we were not allowed to remove a single apple off the tree. We were only allowed to go in and pick up fallen fruit.

So I took piles of damaged apples. Boiled and boiled them with cloves and the peel of oranges and lemons, just as Gran would have done. When the fruit had boiled into a mush, I poured it into an old pillowcase which I then tied to the handle of a broom placed across two chairs. The result was the most delicious jelly. What wonderful things we had from the neighbours' waste.

Our clothes may have come from jumble sales, but I always maintained that food was very important, for

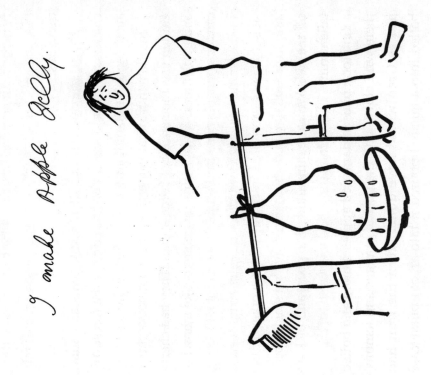

I make Apple Jelly.

some day when our luck changed we must be healthy to enjoy it, as Gran had always said.

When we left London, Rita Webb had said farewell with a large earthenware cooking pot wherein I would casserole meat with all sorts of vegetables. Yet we ate very little meat. Our daily diet was a large bowl of soup made of carrots, onions, celery and lentils, topped with cheese and parsley. With chunks of fresh bread and butter it made a great meal. And so cheap. It is still one of my favourites.

Every day I baked cakes, often with the eggs from the neighbours' hens. Robert loved the rich fruit cake and I always had one standing by.

Once, when he was two years old, I saw him trying to cut a piece himself. So I went and leaned over him, saying, 'Let me cut that.' 'No,' he cried, throwing up his arms and stabbing me in the eye. It was a tomato knife with a pointed tip. Afterwards, when the wound had healed, it was examined in the eye department of the London Hospital, where they would not believe I could still see. 'It's a miracle,' they said, 'it's a miracle.'

Sometimes I have done some odd and wasteful things in spite of myself; against my will, even. In the tangled garden the waist-high grass, the perfumed roses and mock orange all grew rank and wild, and with such speed that you could almost hear it, like a tick from pursed lips.

Here I set up a table for tea. I dragged my oval inlaid table from Portobello Road days to under the old pear tree, where we had tea in the sun-soaked garden. When I glimpsed it from the house, it looked like an Impressionist painting. So I left it there.

The rain came, the hot sun, the frost and the snow. The seasons gradually lifted up the inlay, made the veneer stand on end, separated the wood. And I watched it die. Like a torturer over their victim. But each stage was as beautiful as the last. In the end I painted the skeleton white.

It's a good job I hadn't still got the Dutch marquetry, as those two pieces had gone long ago to pay the rates.

A woman who worked for others

In 1972, Mike Leigh came to see me, and we sat under the old pear tree. He told me that Tony Garnett wanted him to do an improvised film for the BBC. It was the days of 'Play for Today', like *Cathy Come Home* and *Spend, Spend, Spend*. An improvised play seemed very daring. I tried not to think about it because so many dreams never come true.

But of course, it never left my head and when the time

came to sign for the Butlin's season, I told them I couldn't go in case the Mike Leigh job really happened.

'Of course, it won't happen,' they said, 'you won't hear from him again. Besides, you *must* come this year. Equity minimum has gone up to eighteen pounds.' It

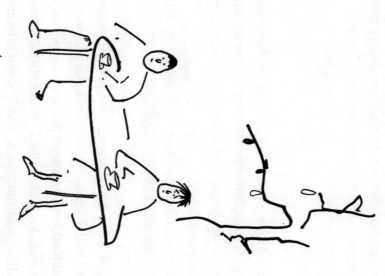

mike leigh came to talk about a woman who worked for others.

was tempting. I had never earned more than thirteen pounds a week with them. But I stuck with my hopes and waited.

It happened. The contract for *Hard Labour* arrived through the post on New Year's Eve. It had been snowing heavily and had settled deep. Everywhere the forest looked magical, the branches all hung low with snow. Then the sun came out and lit the whole scene up with diamonds.

And I had a contract.

I sensed that, with the New Year, new things were happening for me. There was a feeling of change – a change at last for the better – and I felt strangely happy. But here's a funny thing.

During all those years of going to auditions at the RSC, the National Theatre, the Old Vic, the BBC, everywhere, it had always been rejection. And, yet again, at the same time that I was preparing to do Mike's film and had a contract from him, I received a rejection from the BBC for an audition I had done way back.

Anyway, Mike thought I would fit the character of the mother and told me to think about a woman who worked for others. Like a slave. All his characters started by thinking of someone then developing it from there, so I must find a woman who did for others, did everything – cleaned, cooked, cared for.

I chose Mrs Flynn over the road. She did for, she was jolly, went to jumble sales – came to mine in the garden – bought glinty earrings and pretty handbags with flowers on.

Wrong. I got it wrong. Wrong type of woman. I had to learn.

I had to be a Catholic. This meant many weeks attending classes for would-be converts to the Catholic faith. At the end of that time it had been hammered into my head why I had to sacrifice my life for the benefit of others, because of Jesus. At that point I dared to enter a strange church and go to confession. The priest did not scream at me through the grille, 'You are an impostor. I can see through you.' I came out feeling quite weak. I was beginning to know her.

The day came when I went to Manchester to start work. We were to do eight weeks of improvisations, followed by four weeks' filming.

Mike took me to a little second-hand clothes shop and bought me a coat for half a crown. I had got a pair of boots for two pence from a jumble sale. The BBC wardrobe supplied an ancient blue hat of suitable sadness.

We were based in an enormous Territorial Army

depot with vast, rough, oily, mucky concrete floors. This space was divided up into the homes of the various characters. So here we came and did our own thing. Wherever I was, I must do what she would do. I cleaned and shopped and cooked, scrubbed floors endlessly. Went home each night with my stockings torn to holes and blood running from my knees. Then some days I would wear her coat and hat and be out on the streets. We went to the market, where I made another of my big mistakes.

The fruit stalls were wonderful, and so cheap. I couldn't get over the prices. A mountain of waxy lemons grabbed me. I bought a dozen. Mike was angry with me. He went red in the face.

'She would *never* buy a dozen lemons, only one. Only one lemon at a time.'

Mike in the crowd around the stalls. Mike popping up around the empty boxes. Mike's dark eyes, everywhere. It was the same in the fire-stock shop where there were rows and rows of garments that had been singed by fire. Polly Hemingway, as my daughter, was trying to persuade me to buy her a coat that wasn't too badly burned, for £5. The salesman worked in a frenzied effort to get a sale. And Mike was in all sorts of places between the hanging garments.

I went to buy half a pound of tomatoes. The man

135

threw the bag at me. 'Gerrum yourself,' he said. 'Gerrum yourself.'

The family lived in a little house in Salford, and it felt like our home, not a film location. It was in the tightly packed winding streets that have gone now to make way for a very smart new area and the Lowry Centre. It's all shining and fashionable now, but then the old terraces with their back alleys were strung with washing and resounded with children playing.

One day of our filming was interrupted by the constant barking of a dog. Mike had to ask the owner if she could calm it down and keep it quiet. An upstairs window was flung open and her red, furious face looked down into our yard. 'You don't keep a dog and bark yerself,' she shouted.

Another day we were on the streets. I was standing at a pretend bus stop, wearing my penny boots and forlorn hat and coat – looking just as awful as anybody could look. Mike was over the road peering from some doorway with his gimlet eyes.

Suddenly, an Irish labourer stood before me. As big as a house, he planted his feet in his mud-covered boots firmly on the ground. He was wearing his builder's donkey jacket, an old woollen hat, and had several days' growth of beard.

He looked at me with his kind eyes.

'Will you be my woman?' he said.

I didn't invite him back to our base, but maybe I should have done.

My son was played by Bernard Hill and in the film he married Alison Steadman. After the film, Mike married Alison.

Eventually, *Hard Labour* came out early in 1973 on the BBC. I consider it to be one of the best of Mike Leigh's works. Yet when there is a review or retrospective of his work, this film is rarely mentioned. It's all in there. There is not an uncomfortable wrong moment.

Thanks, Mike. If it were not for that film I would still be leaning on my Zimmer frame, serving in some shop.

After that, I dared to approach another agent. I chose to ask one of the best at that time, Al Parker, and I was accepted with warmth and a welcome. By then I was fifty years old.

Dream that I am home again

Our house near Epping sometimes had a life of its own. The two bedrooms at the back, overlooking the forest, had a communicating door where a ghost walked at night. People were known to run out screaming in terror at three in the morning.

Robert slept in one of those back rooms and, being so young, was completely unperturbed by the gentleman he was sure sat in the Lloyd Loom chair at the side of his bed.

Once, when I was sleeping in the other one, an owl was trapped in the chimney. I heard this awful beating noise and a heap of rubble came crashing down several nights in a row. One morning I threw open the door and there on the dressing table sat an enormous tawny owl. Slowly, he turned his head and looked at me.

I went over and opened the window wide. 'Go now,' I said, and he swept past me into the forest. Ever since, I have loved owls and regard them as a symbol of good luck.

Another time I was sleeping downstairs in the little back room with the low window, which looked directly out on to the old pear tree. It looked wonderful in the early mornings when there was fog. Often I would wake and see in the pale mist a couple of cows, their faces pressed against the window, regarding me solemnly with their big sad eyes.

It was some ancient tradition of Epping Forest that gave people the right to let their cattle roam. I think it ended because of the traffic. They no longer roam the gardens, but to this day I believe there is a commoner's

I woke to find two cows looking through the cow window.

right to have cattle in Epping Forest, though behind fences now. At that time, they wandered into any garden they could and ate the roses. Of course, most houses had very well made fences to keep them out, but my wild patch was very accessible. And they couldn't harm the 'lawn'. Children played hide and seek in it.

Once, in the night in the small back room, I rose above my body and saw myself sleeping on my bed. I drifted down the hall, then down the front path under the orange blossom trees to the front gate, where I stopped and realized I was not ready. It was not time. So I went back.

There was a Victorian wooden porch on the front of the house. The door had the original huge iron knocker from about 1840. Every now and then, during the night, some-

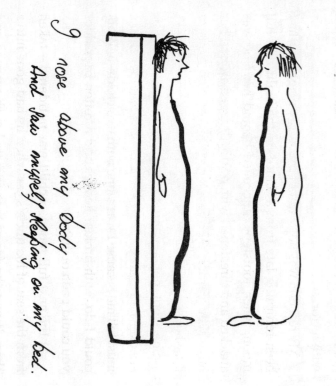

I rose above my body
And saw myself sleeping on my bed.

thing or someone would slam that knocker so hard I had to answer it. No matter how exhausted I was or how deeply I was asleep, I had to open the door and look out into the night. But there was never anyone on the doorstep.

Whatever presence there was in that place, it was benign; there was no threat in it. Threats came from human beings. Creeps. Creeps that snuck around just outside my hedge and filled me with fears. Sometimes, I would switch off all the lights in the house, then peer out through the little lavatory window and almost faint with terror.

My reaction was not without cause. My neighbour had been returning late from a dance on the night of a full moon, when footsteps quickened behind her. She was attacked and threatened with death, dragged around her huge wild garden with its stagnant pond and ruins of glasshouses.

She slept not a wink for more than a week. The attacker had warned her to tell no one, but she felt she must tell me because I was alone with two children. What could I do, with broken hedges and a rotten back door you could push open?

At the next full moon, a child was murdered – taken from the seat of his uncle's car when he had gone into a shop. It was the forest that attracted such warped and evil minds, its ancient trees with their massive growth and the huge bushes suitable for creeps to hide in and bodies from gang murders to be buried.

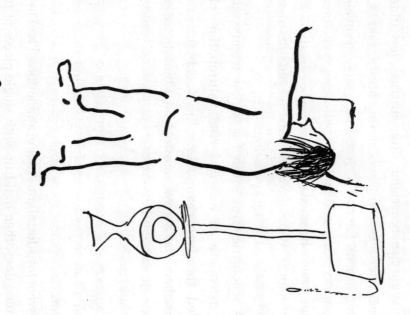

I peered out through the lavatory window.

Restoration

The children were growing up. Robert was in his final year at King Edward's School in Surrey. Sarah shared a flat with her boyfriend, Ron. During my time in Manchester when we were filming *Hard Labour*, I had rented a small flat and cooked for myself each evening, eating too much and drinking too much wine. When the filming was finished, I was overweight and full of rheumatism. Walking down steps was hell, as red-hot knives stabbed at my knees. I was a mess.

A schoolfriend of Sarah's was now training to be an osteopath at a wonderful naturopathic place called the Tyringham Clinic in Buckinghamshire. Tyringham was a great country house built by Sir John Soane. It had not been open as a clinic so very long, and was fresh with all its wonderful ideas. There were no ladies posing around in elegant leotards, but people from all over the world who had come to be made better.

I went for a fortnight. After examinations, I had to fast for nine days, then build up with single pieces of fruit. Every day was filled with treatments like pool exercises, massage, acupuncture, seaweed and steam baths.

I arrived home after that fortnight completely

renewed. I had lost one and a half stone, and my rheumatism had gone to sleep. I was a new woman.

Sarah and Ron

Sarah married Ron in deep winter weather in 1973. I covered the big old table with a lace cloth that was really a Victorian bedspread I had bought for sixpence from a jumble sale.

There was a huge salmon from David's fish shop down the road in the centre of the table, and the room was filled with the scent of food and wine. Sweet-smelling logs burned in all the grates, upstairs and down. Everywhere were bunches of pale-yellow spider chrysanthemums.

Outside, in the darkening sky, the huge ancient trees tossed and turned and made the wedding reception very cosy.

Soon, Eliza and Alexander were born, and made me a happy grandmother.

Over hill and dale

At around this point, I did just one episode of *Last of the Summer Wine*. I went up to Yorkshire to be a housekeeper to Compo, played by Bill Owen. It was sad when Bill died, but fitting that his real-life son Tom came into the series to play Compo's long-lost son.

Anyway, back in the 1970s Compo had advertised for a housekeeper, and I arrived on a bus with all my worldly possessions in a paper carrier bag. I was wearing a very short skirt, long white boots and a blond wig. I was a real tarty piece and I was loving it.

Playing the downcast, put-upon mother in *Hard Labour* with such intensity for so long had reduced me to a sad state. That's what parts do if they are too suffering and deeply felt – they take you down with them. And that's why I love playing nutty creatures in eccentric outfits.

Compo took me to have a feast of chips and mushy peas in that same little café that is in *Last of the Summer Wine* to this day. It was all fine and easy up in Holmfirth in Yorkshire, where it was set, and it was not until we got to the studios back in London that I felt I had so much to learn.

I had no idea what it was really like to be in a sitcom. First of all we had to rehearse for the week and do any scenes on location, like the ones in Holmfirth. Then, we had to act the other scenes in a studio in London before an audience.

What a day that was – still is, I'm sure.

We arrived in the morning, rehearsed this, then rehearsed that – which usually meant different camera angles. A break, then a full dress rehearsal, and another break, perhaps for supper. And then, when you are totally exhausted and have peaked for the day, it's time to begin.

The audience arrives in droves. Hundreds and hundreds of them all ready for a good night out. They get entertained by a warm-up comedian, and his bit is usually packed so full of jokes and hilarity that everyone is worked up into a fine state of laughter and anticipation.

As his performance draws to an end, the warm-up man proceeds to bring in the cast of the sitcom, one by one, and introduce them, in a spotlight, to the excited audience.

We, the cast, dressed in all our character outfits, have been hiding behind screens at the side of this huge studio, and now we are expected to come running out waving and smiling at the audience with a silly look on our faces.

And it was at this point, when I did it for the first time, that I suddenly felt very odd. I came out from behind that screen when he shouted my name, and my legs had suddenly gone stiff. I was wearing my blond wig and the white boots, but my legs had turned into two sticks of wood that wouldn't bend in the middle.

It *was* then that I felt I was a stranger in a new world, and had such a lot to learn. My experience with Mike and all the improvisations had not prepared me for this. I was right back at the beginning. Just as my character had arrived in the bus, so she left in the bus at the end of the episode; and never came back again.

One batty family

I was sent to a meeting at the BBC, who were putting on a new comedy series to be called *I Didn't Know You Cared*. I met the writer, Peter Tinniswood, in the office. He sat there with his quiet smile and the eternal pipe jammed against his teeth. I had gone to be any character in the story he was writing, about the Brandon family. Peter decided I could be Mrs Brandon, the mother of this nutty lot.

The Brandon family lived in Peter's head. He wrote books about them, and now he was doing a comedy series. The books about Mr and Mrs Brandon, their son Carter and the dog are wonderful.

Upstairs in the attic sleep Mrs Brandon's brother Mort and little Uncle Staveley, who wears a small cardboard box around his neck containing the ashes of his friend from the trenches in the First World War. When Auntie Lil sleeps there at the age of nearly seventy, she conceives a child which has a very large head and can communicate by thought.

They have lovely wacky adventures, except the baby with the big head. Sadly, it was considered too delicate to use a character like that then, yet it seems anything goes now – the more lurid, the better.

So we made the series with Robin Bailey as my brother Mort, Stephen Rea as Carter, Anita Carey as his wife, John Comer as Mr Brandon, and little Staveley was played by Bert Palmer.

Every episode took us to a different setting. We had glorious outings to museums, river trips, pub trips, works outings with brass bands, and anywhere that was offbeat.

I didn't wear a blond wig for Mrs Brandon, but grew my own hair long and wore it in a crazy beehive, which was different for me because wigs are my favourite things. I think they define a character right away – even wearing a bald wig does it.

As Mrs Brandon had awful taste in clothes, I could have my fling. Nothing was too wild for her – it was like being a child again and dressing up. I could wear anything, so long as it was in bad taste. In fact, they even allowed me to knit my own jumpers because they could not find anyone else to knit them so badly.

Bird Alone

Another thing I did, which was never completed because it was too naughty, was called *Bird Alone*. It was a TV pilot with me as mother to Yootha Joyce. It was beautifully written by Hugh Leonard, so you had wonderful, real dialogue. It opened with a court scene where Yootha's character was being divorced, with John Le Mesurier as the judge.

The description I gave to the judge, of talking to Yootha behind the dress shop she owned while she was 'carrying on!', was considered too shocking to go out.

Memories of Thora

A series I only appeared once in was *In Loving Memory*. It was a very popular TV show in which Thora Hird ran a funeral business.

I appeared as the owner of a rival firm and the scene we loved so much was when we sat together, curled up in the back of a hearse. And in case we did not look ridiculous enough, I put my hat on back to front. This really touched Thora's funny bone. She never got over it and we laughed about it for the rest of her life.

We met quite often because we both belonged to SAGE, 'Stage for Age'. It's a support branch of Help the Aged.

When Thora came to the committee meetings of this group, we knew we were in for a good time. Her wise-cracks and jokes came streaking down the table like lightning.

When I went to her memorial service in Westminster Abbey in 2003, towards the end of the service the doors burst open and in marched the Salvation Army band playing triumphantly. It was a touching reminder of her work in the TV show, *Hallelujah!*. There wasn't a dry eye in that packed church.

Thora was such a very brave person. She spent her

final years in a wheelchair. She had had hip replacements over the years until there was hardly any bone left, so she had a lot of metal in her poor old legs. This must have caused so much pain, but there was never a moan from her, not a word. It was only another thing to joke about – what she would call her 'tin legs'.

No pig

One day I received a script for a film called *A Private Function* written by Alan Bennett. I had a look at it and it was one of those magic reads, where you could just feel the words dripping off your lips. Not that I would have a lot of words, as the part I was up for was a dumb old mum. It was not yet an offer, but I could not bear to lose it anyway.

I knew where Alan lived in Camden Town, so I asked Robert to go right away and put a postcard through his door, begging and begging that I might do it. I don't suppose Alan was doing the casting, but joy of joy, I was given the part of Maggie Smith's mother.

A Private Function was made in Ilkley, and is a glorious tale of northern life soon after the war. It is still loved to this day.

Maggie's husband, played by Michael Palin, was a chiropodist, and there was a whole list of other beautiful British actors in it too: John Normington, Alison Steadman, Richard Griffiths, Denholm Elliott, Amanda Gregan, Bill Paterson, Jim Carter and Pete Postlethwaite to name but a few. The wonderful people of Ilkley appeared in the shots and lent us costumes from their own theatre.

The plot concerns a pig that had to be the main course at a private function, so the film became known as the pig picture and the animal part was played by twin pigs both called Betty.

Round and round the house they charged, biscuits rapidly disappearing into their mouths at one end and just as rapidly reappearing at the other. To solve this problem, a schoolboy had the job, as work experience, of following Betty with a bucket and a roll of kitchen towels. I wonder what he is doing today, twenty years on. A different job, I hope. But I'm sure both Betties were clean and amiable souls at heart.

It was sad that a less pampered pig had to die, for the dead pig. I hate animals being ill used for a film, but I expect this one just came from the local butcher's.

In the book of the film, with the printed script, Alan Bennett writes that one of his favourite scenes was cut from the film. It featured me sitting on a lavatory, looking sadly at the dead pig lying in the bath. Too sad and gruesome to show, I bet.

Right place, wrong time

The job following that film was a play at the Strand Theatre called *Why Me?*, starring Richard Briers. It was during rehearsals for this play that *A Private Function* had its opening night. This was to be in Leeds because it is so close to Ilkley, and Alan comes from there.

The mayor was going to be there, no doubt wearing his gold chain, so it was going to be a big do. I was given time off from rehearsals to go up and attend the opening, and I asked my daughter Sarah if she would like to come with me.

By this time she was a divorced mother of two. So she made elaborate arrangements to have the children cared for, then picked me up after rehearsals at the theatre. It was a bitterly cold night and snowflakes were already drifting.

We got on the train, and the nearer we drew to Leeds, the harder the snow fell until it became a howling blizzard. It pounded against the windows and screamed across the countryside. Arriving in Leeds, we fought our way around the corner to the Queen's Hotel where we were due to stay, and fell thankfully into the reception area.

'Is anyone here yet?' I said.

'Who?' they asked.

'For the opening of the film,' I said.

'What film?'

'*A Private Function*,' I said. 'It's tomorrow.'

'Oh no, it's not. It's next week.'

Next week.

I picked myself up off the floor and we went into the dining room. We had baked cod with parsley sauce and mashed potatoes, followed by treacle sponge and plenty of custard. Then out into the night again and back to London.

I never got to the opening night because the following week was too close to the opening of the play and I was not allowed to leave. The film opened in London in November 1984.

Argentine adventure

I received a script for a film in Argentina. Now this sounded a bit tricky, because this country had not long ago been involved in the Falklands War.

I arrived at Heathrow to meet Dora Bryan, who was to be my fellow actor. We were to play sisters in a film called *Apartment Zero*. I had never met Dora, only knew she was a household name from her glittering years in revues and the film *A Taste of Honey* in 1961, for which she received a BAFTA award. She was there waiting with her husband Bill. Dora has worked all over the world, but Bill is always with her. So she constantly has a companion and, in this country, her dog is waiting for her in her dressing room too.

Because of the recent conflict, a British plane could not set down in Buenos Aires, as we were still enemies. So first of all we must fly to Paris and go to Rio on a French plane. Flying south from Paris to Rio, we were fed the most brilliant meals non-stop, all beautifully presented and irresistible. I was already overweight but could not stop myself eating the gourmet dishes dripping with butter and cream.

At Rio we changed on to a Brazilian Airlines plane. If possible, their meals were even better, even richer.

There was a tropical storm, and the plane rocked and rattled all the way down the continent. It seemed that the outside shell would blow off. To console myself, I kept on eating. When I emerged at Buenos Aires, I was fat and bloated and feeling very delicate. The storm had not abated. The temperature was ninety degrees, the sky was almost black and the rain came down in sheets.

Because the film was on a very tight budget we were moved to a downtown hotel. The swimming pool where Bill had dreamed of sitting while we were at work was just a dirty hole filled with debris. Work was going on in downstairs rooms night and day, so it was twenty-four hours of hammering. No sleep and no communication. Everyone spoke Spanish and nobody was on time.

One day I went for a medical, for insurance purposes. But, as usual, no one turned up. After a long wait, I blew my top and threw my handbag against the wall. I was pretty near having a stroke. I discovered later that whatever happens, you must keep calm. Don't scream. Don't shout. It's bad for your blood pressure. I moved to a room in a very quiet hotel with no large public rooms. And I stopped eating fat.

The new hotel was near the Recoleta area which was a place I grew to love, and I went there whenever I could. It was there I calmed down.

There was a great expanse of gardens surrounded by high-quality restaurants. In the centre, a huge church by the side of a famous cemetery with avenues of tombs including that of Eva Perón. I felt safe and quiet sitting with all the other grannies in the children's play enclosure. I loved it when all the young people brought their wares to sell and made a market. Jewellery, drawings so witty and so sophisticated, musical instruments and anything else they had made.

Once, after I had slept for a while, I had this urge to go out at midnight. There was a bright moon and it was light as day. A young student stood in the middle of the Recoleta with a telescope, charging a few coppers to look at the stars. Such a joy, and yet he would not take one tiny coin more than he was asking.

It became such a calming experience, and what was wonderful was that Dora and Bill did not neglect me. Of course, they had each other and could have gone off together, but they didn't. We had many meals at the lovely restaurants surrounding the Recoleta.

We saw the mothers wearing headscarves and carrying photographs of their lost children, and saying, 'Where are our children?' We felt the menace of the police quarters when we went there on film business.

Filming started at noon and sometimes went on till the next morning. There would be a long dinner break late in the evening with me, Dora and Bill in our caravan. There was always much food, much wine and lots of talk in many languages.

Then, slowly, all the cast would reassemble and

filming would continue until the early hours, until breakfast if necessary.

Except one night when it did not start again because
the crew refused to go on. They were due to start a crowd
scene on the stairway of the apartment block and a lot of
extras had been engaged. Amongst the extras, the crew
had spotted a man known to have been one of the tor-
turers from the prison. This is not to forget that at the
time the film was made there were terrible happenings in
Argentina and the disappearance of so many, mostly
young, people.

There were groups on the street corner with large
notices saying 'Give back the Malvinas.' We nipped
round there pretty quickly.

Apartment Zero is about the goings-on in an apartment
block, the owner of which was played by Colin Firth. He
gave a wonderful performance, directed by Martin
Donovan, who for many years had been first assistant to
Visconti.

The film came out in 1988 and I love it, as it is full of
personality, intrigue and revenge and shows all the
excitement of that great city, Buenos Aires. And yet, here,
because a particular film critic didn't care for it, it only
appeared for a brief time at one offbeat cinema and did
not get distribution.

Brighton belles

After *Apartment Zero*, I got into the habit of going to Brighton to see Dora. She lived in a huge property on the seafront which Bill was making into flats. I stayed at the back of the house, which overlooked the garden and was directly over the swimming pool.

The garden, too, was huge, with an aviary full of birds and a parrot called Charlie that flew free. Bill's passion is gardening, so it was always a sight to behold, an absolute riot of colour. The pool noises below were lyrical. Joyful echoes of people's voices and the music they played to swim to. Then they would come out and sit in the garden under the window, chatter and drink coffee.

Any moment I could decide to go down and join in, and they would accept me and tell me all their different stories. Then I could have a swim. The pool was warm for people with rheumatism or a bad heart, and they would put on music of your choice for you to swim to. The comfort didn't end there. For round the pool there were rooms let to therapists who did beauty treatments, first-class massage and reflexology.

It was like a health spa. I would come home so refreshed. Oh dear, I can hardly bear to write about it because it all passed, as everything does, and it was sublime. Quite how wonderful it was was hard to realize at the time, but that is always the way. You do not know how good a thing is until it's gone.

I still love going to Brighton, as it does not die in the winter. They have done so much work on the seafront, it is a joy to walk along there and see something different all the time.

One of my favourite spots is around the fish museum, where they sell fish so fresh it nearly jumps out of the pan. I have seen Japanese people take out a knife and make sushi on the spot to eat on the beach. There you are greeted with a smile and maybe a cup of tea. Sit on an upturned boat and hear fishermen's tales. Buy jellied eels, eat prawns and whelks and fly the British flag on the little white-painted stall.

It's right on the seafront where a service is held each year to bless the fish, and many mackerel are eaten. It's a long straight walk from the marina right along to Hove.

Another of my favourite things is to sit on the beach by the West Pier. Although every time I go there, another piece of the pier has disappeared, carried away by a storm. I like it now, just a skeleton out at sea like some piece of sculpture. I wish it would stay like that and not get washed away any more, but be there for the millions of starlings that swoop and sway around it at the same time every night.

Our Betty

Opposite the West Pier. Brighton.

Rich rewards

In 1985, we took the play *Why Me?* for previews in Brighton and Richmond, where it did very well. Eventually the night came to open at the Strand Theatre, and for the first and only time I had my name outside in lights. I was so proud, I nipped outside with a camera.

Amazingly, on that very same night, the BAFTA awards were to take place, and I was up for an award for best supporting actress in *A Private Function*.

So, as the curtain came down on the play, there was a taxi waiting at the stage door to take me to Grosvenor House where the awards were held. I had missed the early presentation in the cinema, and just made it to the award-giving in the ballroom.

I started to guess I had won when they cleared the way for me to go to the platform. Maggie Smith won the Best Actress award. I won Best Supporting Actress.

It was a day spent in a dream. I was so used to being thrown out of agents' offices and having my photographs returned with no reply, yet here I was in a play in the West End with my name in lights outside so that all the people waiting for a bus could see it.

As if that wasn't enough, I was wearing my pale-blue dress trimmed with crystals, standing on the same platform as Princess Anne and receiving a prize. I made a thankyou speech and thought, Is that how you would do it in Hollywood? But I didn't cry, as they often do at their awards. Cry? I just wanted to laugh.

What a day that was, yet already I had my OAP's bus pass.

Robert and Sara

Another delightful occasion came in 1985, when my son Robert married Sara Keene. Sara set up a partnership with Ginger Corbett and always seemed to be going off to China to do the public relations on Bertolucci's *Last Emperor*, though she said it was only twice.

I was most impressed by anyone going to China to do a job – I had grown up thinking it was a big adventure to go on an evening trip to Cleethorpes for a shilling.

But Sara came back and first Tom, then Leo, were born. What a joy it is to have grandchildren around as you get older.

Stage for Age

While I was working in *Why Me?*, Richard Briers had to attend a big event for Help the Aged. Being such a warm and charming person, he is always much in demand for charities, and he asked me to go along with him. That day they were launching an appeal for an alarm for elderly people to wear around the neck and press if help was needed.

It was shortly afterwards that Nicola McAuliffe and Robert Powell created the theatrical branch called SAGE (Stage for Age), where we do many things to support Help the Aged. Princess Diana was the patron.

For me, this led to something else. When I was asked on one occasion to read in York Minster, it struck me that it looked a long way down the aisle to the door and I wondered if I could make my voice carry that far? In the far distance I could see the first aid man sitting there, so I directed my words to him – and they made it!

I was delighted, and it gave me confidence to read in many different places for different charities. Mostly at Christmas, I have read in great places like the Guildhall, St Martin-in-the-Fields and the Festival Hall.

And of course, this does mean more clothes. I am always thrilled to go out and buy another outfit. It's the same kind of excitement as being five years old and prancing around in an old curtain.

Working with Les

La Nona is a wonderful story set in Argentina, about a family that emigrated from Italy to Buenos Aires. The head of the family is an old woman, 'La Nona', who is a hundred years old. She eats them out of house and home – in fact, she eats them out of life, for one by one they die. I was to play her seventy-year-old daughter, Anula.

It was a great story and a great cast – Jim Broadbent, Tim Spall, Sue Brown, Jane Horrocks, Maurice Denham and Stephen Warbeck. And the old woman to be played by none other than the famous comedian, Les Dawson.

It was part of the performance season directed and produced by Simon Curtis. When the day came to start we all arrived in good time at the rehearsal rooms in White City, and sat around the table, agog. Eyes turned towards the door. Then it flew open and in bounced Les like the star he was, straight off the plane from Blackpool.

A fat man in a turquoise jumpsuit all aglitter with diamonds and a big, big smile.

Les was great to work with. He bonded everyone into a great big happy bunch. No sitting around in a corner on your own. The rehearsals went ahead and we had wigfittings and dress-fittings. Then came the day when Les went off to be dressed.

Out of the door went diamond-sparkling, droll, witty Les and in walked a hundred-year-old woman in a long black dress, hair with centre parting and a low bun. Scowling, teeth champing for all the foods he was about to eat, eyes darting here and there, looking for the next thing to grab.

One by one she destroyed us. I died drinking poison that had been intended to get rid of her. She even ate the flowers from my coffin.

And I banged my leg so hard when I fell that I had a nasty lump for days, but I was told I had to do the dying fall again, because the first time you could see I was wearing black knickers and Anula would not wear black knickers. But Anula did have golden hair, which meant another blond wig.

By now, I had begun to fancy myself in a blond wig so much, I vowed I would grow my hair into that shape and as I got more and more grey I would go more and more blonde. So that's what I did, and as the

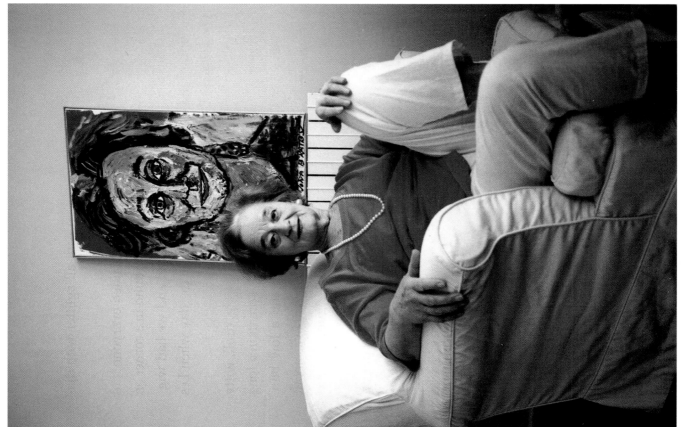

The John Bratby portrait

With grandson
Tom in 1987

18

My colleagues
Peggy Mount and
David Aston on the
radio show, *The Old
Ladies at the Zoo*

19

Les Dawson was the mother in *La Nona* in 1991

Grandma Pirate in a fine children's series called *Pirates* in 1994

At a Help the Aged Christmas event with Diana Moran, June Whitfield, Thora Hird, Jean Anderson and HRH Prince Charles

Playing Letitia Cropley with the cast of *The Vicar of Dibley*

Larking around for Water Aid

Reading for the British Legion at the Guildhall, London

The highlight of my career. The lovely *Royle Family* cast members: Ralf Little, Caroline Aherne, Craig Cash, Sue Johnston and Ricky Tomlinson

On stage in
Endgame with
Geoffrey Hutchins,
Albery Theatre,
2004

At the launch of
*Charlie and the
Chocolate Factory*
with David Morris
in 2005

With my grandchildren in 2005: Leo, Tom, Alex and Eliza

With my self-portrait

years passed and my hair became silver, it was easy.

I do believe Les Dawson would have done a lot more straight acting after *La Nona*, as a change from stand-up comedy, had he lived. He really loved playing that character, and wanted to do more. He would have made a great Falstaff.

The great directors

In 1983 I played Miss Meacham in Terence Rattigan's *Separate Tables*, directed by John Schlesinger, with Julie Christie and Alan Bates as the leads. I felt I had a lot in common with Miss Meacham, who sat agonizingly by herself at her little table, her face dipped into the sporting pages so that no one need say hello.

It is always an inspiration to work with a director of that stature. It can mean at the end of the day you have been made to give your best.

Although it doesn't always work. It depends on the chemistry. I have enormous admiration for Roman Polanski and his brilliant films. I've read his life story and know how he survived the war when he was only a child – incredible.

So when I was to spend a day in Prague doing a scene from *Oliver Twist* with him, I was very excited. But alas, I was glad when that day was over. I didn't feel I had done my best.

I also went to Prague for the version of *Oliver Twist* written by Alan Bleasdale, directed by Renny Rye. In this version, which was shown on ITV in 1999, I was the old woman who was there at the birth of Oliver and stole the locket from the young mother.

We had the most wonderful locations for this. To film, we would go far out into the countryside, to old monasteries, huge, dark and grey, in places we would never have found as tourists. There would be massive empty spaces full of shadows and dust to be turned into long dormitories for orphans, or to accommodate food-laden tables where the workhouse board could meet. And the heavy outside walls could serve well as a Victorian street in the East End of London.

At times, as we worked around the place, there would be the tolling of a bell and a group of sweet-faced young girls in their nuns' habits would skip past into a side chapel. Then we could hear them singing wistful songs to Jesus behind screens.

The birth of Oliver was done in the Barrandov Studios in Prague, which were the ones used by Hitler to make his propaganda films when he overran Czechoslovakia. Of course, I was in the scene because I had to steal the locket when the girl died.

There were numerous small children in the film. It was sad to see so many people holding infants, from newborn to toddlers, hoping to get a job. They were from local orphanages, melancholy little infants, all there with a view to earning the odd penny towards their keep.

Even in the face of a very young child you can read anxiety, and to have cast the big, pink bouncing babies we see all around us would have been wrong for the film. The baby used for the birth scene was very young and extremely small. My heart was in my mouth all the time the scene took to complete. The tiny thing looked as if he had just been born, yet he was probably ten days old. We had to apply made-up smears of blood, which made him slippery.

Everybody sweated. Sophia Myles, who played the young mother, agonized as much as if she had really given birth to him. But the doctor, played by Michael Bertenshaw, handled him so well that the scene was completed safely. What a relief when it was over.

Twice I have removed the sheets from Scrooge's bed. I seem to be a Dickens type. Added to my times in *Oliver*

Twist, I have been in *A Christmas Carol* twice and played the part of Peg Sliderskew in *Nicholas Nickleby* more than once.

I really can't remember how many of these old hags I have played. I've enjoyed them. But I've also had quite long periods of disappointment that I did not get more interesting parts at a time when I could have done them.

Song and dance

To my amazement, I was actually in a musical. I only have a music-hall singing voice and have memories of long ago singing 'Next Monday Morning Is My Wedding Day' on the stage at the Unity Theatre.

Now, I had only one little song in the musical *Cell Block H* at the Queen's Theatre, with Paul O'Grady as Lily Savage. I played Little Lizzie from the TV series, so it wasn't sequin time for me, but it was for Lily Savage. I used to stand beside Paul on the stage and think, My God, what beautiful legs.

He has gone on to do so many different and interesting things, and what I admire about him is that he does so much for animals. In his shows he finds them homes, and when he did that series of travels, especially in the Far East where animals are treated appallingly, he sought out the sad situations and did all he could to right them.

High spirits

When Beryl Reid had an accident, I took her place to play the mother of the wonderful Peter O'Toole in the film *High Spirits*. He was a joy to work with. I was dressed in a long flowing robe and a high silver wig, then he took my hand and led me on to the set. I stumbled a bit with my words in that scene, but he was totally serene and happy and led me on to the right tracks. The film came out in 1988.

I never met Beryl Reid, but played another of her parts when she was not well: in *Apartment Zero*. It's a pity we didn't meet because I feel we would have had a lot in common. Cats, for instance.

One night after she died, I had just dropped into a spiritualist meeting. I was told that Beryl was there and wanted to speak to me about her cats. She had left nine and was very worried about them. I have been unable to do anything about them and I feel I have let her down.

A Victorian whimsy

I must mention a gloriously eccentric film called *Sir Henry at Rawlinson End* which came out in 1980. Sir Henry was played by Trevor Howard. I was Lady Philippa of Staines. Denise Coffey was a mad woman running around the house cooking chips.

The location was Knebworth House, which was supposed to be haunted by a wooden dog. I can remember sitting at the huge dining table in the great hall, dipping my false teeth in champagne. The wooden dog flew in on a wire and, lifting a wooden leg, peed on to the dining table.

The table was in utter confusion. Trevor Howard helping himself to a shot of whisky from a bottle strapped to his wrist and standing beside the writer of the piece, the wonderful Viv Stanshall. At the same time, Viv was holding an old tobacco tin from which he was picking out live worms and stuffing them in his mouth. J. G. Devlin was the butler. It was hilarious.

All the time this was happening, in the gallery above us the tour of the historic house was going on and rather bewildered people were peering down, no doubt thinking they were witnessing a re-enactment of some notable event. Viv was so clever, with his wild imagination.

❀

I remember watching that film in a West End cinema with only about two other people in the audience. But I do believe it exists to this day somewhere, where it is watched with great affection and enjoyment. Perhaps by a film society, or just very discerning people.

Viv used to say to me, 'You live alone? I couldn't live alone. I would never live alone. That's terrible.' But alas, Viv did eventually live alone, in a bedsit, and died when his cigarette set the bedclothes on fire.

First nights

In 1980, I did another Alan Bennett job. I was in his play *Enjoy* at the Vaudeville Theatre. This was a play that did not run long, perhaps because it was too sad and made old people cry. But it has some great moments in it, and maybe too much truth.

Mine was only a small part, of the neighbour next door, but nevertheless, on the first night we all got the same treatment.

First nights in the West End theatres are positively daunting. Apart from learning the lines and having to do the show in front of the critics, some of whom may be famous for tearing you to pieces, you have to worry about the first-night business itself.

The nightmare is: will you be at your best on that night? Have you done the part a hundred times better at the preview? Will you trip up on that loose bit of carpet as you make your entrance? Supposing you are constipated and you are wearing that tight dress. Supposing the cat should be taken ill again. Oh dear, it's all such a nerve-racking business.

But it would be unforgivable to overlook the traditions of the first night, and by hook or by crook you have got to find for everyone in the show a suitable card expressing your love and amazement at their being so brilliantly gifted and so right in the part.

And a gift for everyone. If your part is big, your gift must be – a big bunch of flowers, a big bottle of champagne, a big box of chocolates. Gifts. Gifts. Gifts.

Dressing rooms on a first night are a sight. It's like Christmas. I used to worry so much about getting the right thing, but sometimes when I had splashed out on chocolates and flowers, they hadn't even noticed they were from me. I always thought that a nice bar of soap was a good idea. Good soap in a dressing room is always a pleasure.

So we got to the first night of *Enjoy* at the Vaudeville Theatre, and all the usual stuff, the gifts and so on, are piled up in the corridors. And there is dear Alan Bennett with a heap of carrier bags – he has baked each one of us a fruitcake. With his own two hands he has baked us a cake. And I tell you, it was so good he could make his fortune as a baker if his words ever fail. But they don't show any sign of doing that. Thank heavens.

The theatre is rife with superstition. Dressing rooms are usually full of good-luck symbols, endless cards screaming 'Good Luck' at you, and very often a precious object that must never leave your side or the good times would go with it, like a little teddy bear or a china toad or anything you treasure. Now, I consider that a dangerous thing because you might leave it at home!

STAGE DOOR

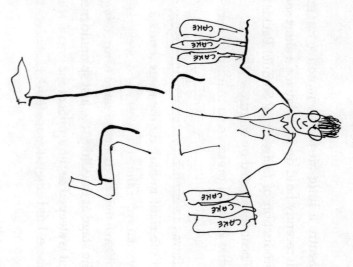

Alan Bennett brings up such a
cake on the first night of 'Enjoy.'

Play time

I find theatre a little bit too demanding for me now, although recently I did do one play for a short season. It was a production of *Endgame* by Samuel Beckett at the Albery Theatre, directed by Matthew Warchus.

A couple of years previous to that I had done a play called *Playhouse Creatures* at the Old Vic in the Peter Hall Season. It was a very good account of the first woman to be given the right to play on the stage in 1660. (Before that only men were allowed.)

Also, it gave me the chance to stand on that wonderful stage. The stage at the Old Vic is just splendid, no doubt because it is steeped in the spirits of the greats who have played there. I did enjoy it, but I think I had decided that I would do no more theatre.

So when I heard about *Endgame* I thought, Oh no, it's theatre. Particularly as the only female part in it is the mother in the dustbin.

'Well,' I said, 'I just couldn't spend the evening in a dustbin.' Me and my claustrophobia. After all, I can't even sit in the middle of a row at the cinema and have to sit on the end seat, so that says something about me. The dustbin was out. So was I. But it didn't go away.

They were extremely kind and said they would cut a

hole in the stage for me where I could pop up, then pop back when I'd finished. After all, it's only one scene.

Furthermore, the dustbins for the parents would be down stage instead of being stuck at the back as they usually are, which meant that they would be so much more part of the main action.

Well, you couldn't get away from generosity like that so I was weakening. But then there was my voice. My voice had always been extremely strong, since the days of the exercises when I was belting it out at the Old Vic. But since then, I didn't think my projection had been that good. I worried. Would it reach?

The Albery Theatre is huge and goes upwards like a tunnel. You have to project to get your voice to the upper layers. Don't I know it! I saw *St Joan* there long ago when I could only afford the cheapest seats, and I was watching the tops of the actors' heads while at the same time holding on to the bar in front of me in case I fell and landed in the pit.

So no. I was sure my voice wouldn't make it now. The next thing, I was taken to the theatre to stand on the stage and recite 'Three Blind Mice' over and over again, aiming my voice at the gods. And it went fine, so that was it.

They were so good to me there, fixing a hydraulic lift under the hole in the stage. I had to stand on the little platform and then, at a signal, it would start to rise and take me up into the dustbin placed over the hole. In the dustbin next to me was Geoffrey Hutchings as my husband. The idea of being tossed up through a hole in the stage would not be a mystery to a pantomime actor – they do it all the time – but it had never happened to me before.

When any scene was over, down went the lift and I was able to disappear to my dressing room, do whatever I liked. Drink tea, eat sandwiches, read the paper or just doze and listen to the play going on over the Tannoy.

Michael Gambon was Hamm. Lee Evans was Clov. I used to sit there feeling grateful that I was not playing Hamm. It must be the most terrifying part to play. To sit there unable to move, in the middle of that great stage. Isolated, and having to act out all that difficult dialogue. Dialogue which to me never seems to link up one thought with the next – not until you are led along as if by a thread, anyway. No, it jumps without warning, all over the place. I don't know how people even learn it. There you are, in the middle of the stage, and if you dry you can't wander over to the prompt corner and whisper, 'What comes next, love?'

Of course, Michael Gambon did it magnificently and I feel sure it was an exceptional production of that extraordinary play.

Backstage tales

Another play I did was J.B. Priestley's *When We Are Married*, at the National Theatre in 1979. I played Mrs Northrop, the daily skivvy in the household. That was a very stylish production directed by Robin Lefèvre.

Between the acts and in the interval, in front of the stage, a small platform rose up from the depths below. On this platform sat the Tiny Winters Trio. They were a delightful addition and spoke exactly the right language for the mood of the play.

They sat on little gilded chairs under palms so it was suddenly a palm court production which must have looked very pretty when the green leaves started to rise up through the floor.

Mrs Northrop is a very boring part, though. It's fine when you are on the stage but between appearances you have long waits until it's time to pop through the door again. It was a long walk back to the dressing rooms at the National Theatre. But what a treat to be in a dressing room! So many in the old theatres are awful. Some have no windows and are really tacky; a lot of bits left in smelly drawers, patches of chewing gum or the odd sock, light-bulbs missing and damp patches.

❧

But these dressing rooms were bright and airy with windows to open. And there were rows and rows of lavatories and showers. Lots of lavatories, that gave me great pleasure. It's the first thing I look for anywhere. The fire escape – then, where's the lavatory? In an old theatre, even if the management has done up your dressing room, given you a sofa or an easy chair and a vase of flowers and there are no missing light-bulbs, the lavatory is often miles away. Miles and miles away. Without a doubt, it will be up or down flights of stairs. There will just be the one solitary loo to be shared by several dressing rooms. The agony then depends on the size of the cast.

Except when they're at the National Theatre, those big musicals always seem to be in old theatres. I wonder how they manage? Up the stairs in some elaborate costume to spend a penny before you go on, only to find a queue, or somebody has dropped something down the pan and it can't be used at all.

In the Albery Theatre, there's a haunted lavatory. It's on stage level so it's very handy, but because of the atmosphere you would only use it in a case of extreme urgency. It's a long passage with the throne at one end, and covering the walls are props from every play that has been put on there. It may be just a cigarette or a glove or a wax flower, but they are all there, dry and dusty, filled with the emotion of a life now over. I could only sit, paralysed, watching in case a hand crept out of the wall to touch a cricket bat or a feather, or in case an eye should be looking through one of the masks. I had to get out of there fast.

Oh the problems, the problems.

Backstage at the National, there was always a bowl of communal sweets. But it was still boring waiting, so mostly I passed the time thinking about Mrs Northrop. Who *was* Mrs Northrop? What would her life be like in the year 1900? Pretty awful, I would imagine. I used to go home with her in my mind and think, When she gets the sack in the play, I'll give her another life after that. Then I wrote it all down, and it was about a woman whose luck comes later in life.

But Mrs Northrop haunted me. I did it again on BBC2, and then was asked yet again to do it on the stage in the West End, but I could not face it. Anyway, I had written her story. It was finished.

House for sale

At this time, I was still in the old house in Epping. I had longed to leave it and had painted a 'For Sale' sign on the back of one of my paintings.

I would sit and brood by the fire and decide I could stand the place no longer, then rush out and hang the 'For Sale' sign in the laburnum tree by the front gate.

After a few more days of brooding, I would rush out and bring it in again, because I knew I could not leave yet. I could not leave a place that paid for the children's education.

This went on for eighteen years, which kept the curtain-twitchers over the road busy wondering whether it was on or off.

We still had a constant stream of cats – strays – and mice. My neighbour Ella Warren had a cat refuge in her garden, so I had jumble sales in mine to raise cat funds. There would be stuff spread around the hedges and flags in the old pear tree.

I would hang a notice in the laburnum tree to say there would be a jumble sale and people would respond magnificently, leaving piles of stuff on the doorstep. All sorts of odd things turned up. Most of it would sell, but one thing that did not sell I found most intriguing. It was a juice extractor from the thirties, a fearsome-looking object made of very heavy metal and with an enormous screw like an old-fashioned sausage machine.

The donor informed me that her aunt had owned it and had survived the years as a prisoner in Auschwitz with the juice extractor by her side. Where, in that place, she found any fruit or vegetables to extract juice from, I do not know. But nobody would buy it, so, desperate to be rid of it, I buried it. It must be there still, in that suburban garden. Maybe it will be dug up in a few hundred years and be found very interesting.

Small notice

Not all the films get the interest they deserve. *We Think the World of You* was one of those. Adapted from the novel of the same name by J. R. Ackerley, it is the story of the rivalry between two men for the love of a dog. It was directed by Colin Gregg, and the two rivals were played by Alan Bates and Gary Oldman. I was Gary's mother and Frances Barber played his wife.

My husband was played by Max Wall. Only a small cast, made smaller by the fact that, in the story, my son is in prison most of the time. No extras to flood the place with bodies. We were just a tiny undisturbed group of players.

The studio was an old pump-house in south London and the layout was very sympathetic and suited our tale. It was a cosy film, no huge exteriors posing lots of problems, and in the long gaps when lights and cameras were being arranged we sat in a corner and talked.

Of course, Max Wall took the chair. His was a story to tell. Max could walk on to a stage on his little knobbly legs, not say a word and bring the house down. He was a character of such magnetic quality that his comedy was totally unique – it was fascinating to hear him tell how it had developed. He hadn't just stood up in a comedy store and been an overnight success: it had taken the best part of sixty years to become the actor he was. Different jobs, starting way back in the Paris circus, all shaped him into the Max Wall legend.

Alan Bates sat quietly by, an actor so assured he did not need to make a display of it. He was always so pleasant and gentle, so easy for us lesser mortals to work with. He would sit and listen a lot to Max telling his tales, of the ups and downs of his life, and how delighted he was now that he had a new studio flat and was buying some pots and pans.

When it was Alan's turn to speak, it was always about his sons. He had twin sons whom he adored. He was so proud of them, they were so handsome and he loved to talk of them.

It was a lovely film that just didn't get around enough.

Pirates

Another forgotten series I did was called *Pirates*, which was for children. There's the rub. So few adults see children's programmes, and I was doing this comedy for about two years.

The story was about a family of pirates who had been sailing round the world for about five hundred years. They had finally decided to be landlubbers, so had bought a house in north London where they carried on with all their naughty pirate ways.

For instance, if they had a quarrel with the neighbours, they would make them walk the plank out of the bedroom window. Their food was disgusting and they ate all kinds of squirmy things cooked by me. I was grandma and head of the family. The squirmy things were made of rubber, but some other things were real. For instance, all the firearms I had to deal with were real antiques and they weighed a ton. Old guns including blunderbusses, swords, all as heavy as lead. I once had to hold a sword so long between my lips, it removed a tooth.

The adventures the pirates had were wonderful, bizarre and exciting. Towards the end I could hardly speak, I was so exhausted. For me, though, the series passed unnoticed. No publicity at all. Nothing, except for a few kids in the street who said, 'Were you the grandma pirate?' I would nod and turn to reply, but already they had gone back to their ice lollies.

The Revengers' Comedies

Before we leave the subject of forgotten films, I must mention *The Revengers' Comedies*. This was based on plays by Alan Ayckbourn about two people who meet on a bridge over the Thames where they have gone to commit suicide.

When I say 'plays', I mean that originally it was two plays done on consecutive nights, but you had to see them both to get the full story. Which I suppose could work out jolly expensive if more than one of you was going to see it. At least it was condensed into the one film.

Malcolm Mowbray, who had done *A Private Function*, directed it. And it had a stellar cast: Sam Neill, Helena Bonham-Carter, Kristin Scott Thomas, Rupert Graves, Charlotte Coleman, John Wood, Anita Dobson, Martin Clunes.

Most of the filming was done in a twelfth-century castle near Oxford, set in the most glorious English countryside.

The hunt came, and there's a sight if ever there was one. The spectacle of the horses and hounds against the background of English landscape is so stunning, it looked grand on the film. Of course, I am not talking about hunting the fox or killing it, just what the hunt looks like, especially the hounds leaping up and down.

I have no idea what happened to the film, which is a shame. I saw it on TV once at about 1 a.m. on BBC2.

The devil is in the detail

Quite different again was a fantastically popular four-part TV drama I appeared in in 1986 called *The Life and Loves of a She-Devil* which was a really splendid story adapted from the novel by Fay Weldon.

It is a story of revenge, in which a big, plain woman has herself surgically reduced by a series of fearsome operations to become the form of her husband's beautiful lady-novelist lover.

The BBC went to town on the whole production, buying a lighthouse on the cliffs next to Beachy Head. Around the base of the lighthouse they built a huge room with windows overlooking the sea and furnished it with exquisite taste. Gardens were laid out. A swimming pool built. Patricia Hodge played the beautiful novelist, Dennis Waterman her lover. His vengeful wife was Julie T. Wallace.

I was mother to the beautiful lady novelist, who kept me in an old people's home doped with sleeping pills, until a nurse played by Miriam Margolyes came along and substituted vitamin pills for the sleeping ones.

So I got to the magic lighthouse and created havoc. I got drunk and drove a white Rolls-Royce nearly over the cliff. What a plot!

I couldn't drive – it was my daydreaming adventures on the old bike that put me off, all those years ago. So the BBC gave me lessons and I learned to drive in the white Rolls-Royce. But of course, when it came to going over the cliff, this was done by a stunt girl wearing my blond wig. What a brave girl! She drove that great car on a single steel rod over the cliff, hung there, rocked it, then slowly reversed. I was almost too afraid to watch. But I did.

What fun it was to play that part. I was really sorry when it ended. I could watch that programme over and over again.

A perpetual feast

Three years later, *The Cook, the Thief, His Wife and Her Lover* was a great success and an extraordinary film, directed by Peter Greenaway. It was an amazing experience just to be on the set.

I did little more than sit around the table, which was dominated by Michael Gambon. His part called for a big actor, and nobody comes bigger. It was a joy to watch it all happen. I played his mother-in-law and could relax enough to look around.

The display of food was like Harrods and Fortnum's rolled into one. The fish display alone could have come from the seven seas. I averted my eyes from that because I thought I saw something move. Maybe it was a crab.

Everything about it was over the top and it pleased me enormously to be there, just to have a look at it and enjoy the scenes. We wore clothes by Jean-Paul Gaultier and I had a brief little nothing with a skirt that consisted of a fringe, like a lampshade. My shoes were just little strappy things with high heels, and it was a long way from the fringe bit to the barely-there shoes.

Now this was one of those big-freeze times. The temperature dropped way below zero. The floor of the great studio was made of concrete and my legs froze, my feet and legs were just numb. Wasn't I stupid? I was sitting with my legs underneath a big solid table. Why on earth was I not wearing fur-lined boots and longjohns and a blanket or two? No one could possibly have seen them if I'd had hot water bottles strapped to my legs. But I couldn't bear the thought of spoiling the Jean-Paul Gaultier look – I got such a thrill from wearing it.

Of course, I paid for my vanity with a large dose of rheumatism and had weird, painful legs for about a year, which meant I had to walk around with cabbage leaves stuffed down my stockings, which is my cure for bad knees.

Peter Greenaway was the quietest director I have known. He stood at the side of the amazing scene he had created and watched. He wore a large tweed overcoat and looked very warm and relaxed. I believe it must be that the people he cast could simply do it, so he let them do it.

Some time afterwards he sent me a script. I was to play a soldier in France in the Thirty Years War. I was thrilled. The part was that of a recorder to stand by the surgeon on the battlefield, and as the dead were brought off, the surgeon operated on them to try and find their souls. His search for human souls went on endlessly. It would have been a wonderful film.

Sadly, it did not get made, but I still have the script and Peter Greenaway's letter.

❦

Nosing around

Twice I played Madam Balls in the *Pink Panther* films. Madam Balls kept the disguise shop with her husband, selling things like humps and bad legs. We sold a hump to Peter Sellers as Inspector Clouseau.

My outfit was in many-layered gypsy style, and my hair was all tangled. But the main asset was the nose. The makeup department of a film of this size never fails to amaze me. When you consider all the effects they can achieve, I suppose my nose was a very small order. All the same, they spent an enormous amount of time and skill on it, and it was a conk of truly bulbous proportions with a large wart at the tip. I still have it in a drawer at home.

It is large and loose and rubbery and I can easily slip it over my own big nose. Then all it needs is a bit of face glue and the transformation is done. So there was I with this nose and Peter Sellers falling about laughing. He fell over the furniture and laughed and laughed.

Not all noses are so kind. I had one made for another film and just as much care was taken to make it. But fitting it was painful because the flaps gripped inside my nose and tore it. That took two visits to the Royal Free Hospital.

It's amazing how many bumps and bangs and hurts you can get on a film set, without it being life-threatening. Wigs, for instance. Wigs can be attached to your head kindly or unkindly. An unkind makeup girl or boy can ruin your stay on a job. If you protest, they say, 'I've got to do it like this. The wig won't stay on otherwise.'

Thank goodness most are very kind. In fact the makeup van is the centre of the community. There you sit in a line at the beginning of your day and have things done to you. It's very nice if it takes a long time. But I have never had to go through the agony of being made up to be a gorilla or the Elephant Man or something from another planet. That must be awful. No, I mean it's nice and soothing. So you can sit there and maybe they'll make you a tea or coffee. It's always warm in the makeup van, no matter what the weather outside, and it's awash with gossip. Never mind if you'll be the subject the minute you're out of the door.

The wardrobe people are equally helpful. They are there beside you in all weathers and will, for instance, lay plastic on the ground to save you sinking into the mud or clay. They will be your friends and allies, but they haven't got a cosy cavern or a sanctuary like the makeup van.

In costume

It has always surprised me how it is possible to appear on the streets of London dressed as anything at all and attract no attention. Up in Camden Town I see so many punk outfits. I am so impressed, I want to stare and stare. I want to examine each colour, each style of makeup, boot, shoe, leather bits, jewellery.

I want to know the inspiration behind this or that choice of design, and I'm thinking that they must be very caring and sincere people to make so much effort with their outfits. But I mustn't stare, mustn't ask questions, because it would be rude. It would be considered a criticism, not approval.

It reminds me of a time fifty years ago, when I worked at the little Gateway Theatre in Westbourne Grove. The theatre was going out on hire to a group of actors coming from Australia to make their mark on London. The play they had chosen was *The Importance of Being Earnest*, but the cast was not quite complete because they did not have a Miss Prism. So they gave me the part. It was some show, with the whole of that classic in broad Australian and a north-country Miss Prism.

They were the dearest people, and we stayed friends afterwards. Don and Cynth were always thinking up new ideas, and wanted to create a children's play about two kangaroos. They came round to my place by the Portobello Road and we made the kangaroo costumes first out of a cotton fabric.

When the cotton fabric looked something like a kangaroo, we then cut it out in a thick brown nylon fur fabric, adding metal claws and nails and a long tail, which was really a wooden stool for them to sit on. When the two outfits were finished, we all went down in a van to do a photo shoot in Kensington Gardens.

Down the path in their outfits come Don and Cynth into the busy scene, and the two kangaroos stand there and pose. But not one person takes a second glance, the conversations just carry on as normal. Heads half turned quickly turn back, as if it's the most ordinary thing in the world to see two huge kangaroos in the park on a bright summer morning.

High-quality productions

Thanks goodness Lynda La Plante took me seriously and gave me a part in *Trial & Retribution* number five in 2002. It was a treat to be so bleak and meaningful in a play of such standing. Everything she writes is top-notch. The standard of her productions is so high.

It is amazing how rough and ready productions can be, even in shows that are popular and have a big following. When you have worked on one of those you come away feeling you have not done your best, thinking, Well, perhaps nobody will notice me.

When I was much younger, I sometimes felt *Hard Labour* had been ignored or forgotten and I had been dropped into the 'toothless old hag' bit of the filing cabinet instead of being considered for characters with more depth. And yet at the same time I am so grateful that I have not grown old doing jobs in shops on my Zimmer frame! Of course I have Mike Leigh to thank for that – who knows? perhaps no one else would have seen any possibilities in me.

When Mike Leigh was making *Secrets and Lies* he asked would I just be one of the customers for the photographer in the film, and pose a bit? I did it, and so did Alison Steadman. Timothy Spall played the photographer.

That was a piece of cake because Timothy Spall is such a wonderful actor as well as an endearing character. I had known Tim for a long time, from way, way back when he was a schoolboy. He came to my house with my son Robert when they were both still at school and attending the National Youth Theatre. Robert went to film school eventually, and asked Tim to be in his student production.

This turned out to be a short film called *Sanscape* and was shot over the Essex marshes. It was full of melancholy and strange light and unfulfilled lives. I was in it, peering through a cottage window along with a wonderful actress called Marilyn Taylerson. Tim wandered through it in a haunted way, and it was really excellent.

We thought that when Tim left school and the National

Youth Theatre he should go on to a drama school. That is just what he did. I do not see him as any different now than then – the same actor with the same lovable qualities.

Writing and painting

Between jobs I love writing down my ideas. Not that I can do it anywhere. I can't. But there's a certain spot on Brighton beach where I can sit on a deckchair under one of the yellow umbrellas and scribble. They say Brighton is on a ley line, and I could believe that – well, the beach might be. I get the same buzz on a little square of beach I know in Spain.

Just a tiny patch of sand on the Costa del Sol, a sunshade and an exercise book, and ideas come to me there. Naturally there's a café within a few sandy steps and the scent of sardines grilling around lunchtime.

Never mind too much scribbling. All my time between jobs should be filled with a paintbrush in my hand, trying to catch up with all the years I have lost.

There were moments when I was young when I did a painting, and then when I looked at it I felt that if I tried for another fifty years I might do one worth looking at.

But now I've neglected it for fifty years, and it's gone. It's left me.

I've had a stab at it now and then. Sometimes it's come out in the style of painters I have scarcely known. Otto Wix was one. I have admired him, but when I went to an art class, the tutor looked at my work and said, 'Oh, Otto Wix did that.' Or, I paint a picture on a huge piece of board, then long afterwards find that Uccello did one just like it around 1450 and made a much better job of it.

Years ago, I did go through a stage when all paintings had to be big. I used to buy sheets of hardboard and treat them. I painted a portrait of a mermaid, sitting there with her floating hair and fishes and with her trophy, the skull of a drowned sailor, on the rock beside her. I liked it. I sent it to an art exhibition and forgot about it.

Then, about ten years later, when I was sitting dreaming, I thought about it. So I wrote and asked if I could collect it. No reply. Now that was to Loughton Library. I mean to say, if you work in a library, you should be able to write a postcard to say, 'It's not 'ere.' But, of course, I expect the people who saw it have left, long ago. And I suspect by now it could be a partition in a chicken run or serving as a roof to an old shed.

In 1985, I was lucky enough to have my portrait

painted by John Bratby. He wrote to me on his beautiful, flower-decorated writing paper, to ask me for a sitting. It was an adventure to go to his amazing octagonal house by the sea, stacked with hundreds of paintings.

He was lively and entertaining, and his wife Patti supplied an endless choice of sandwiches. I had to wait two months to collect the portrait because the paint was so thick, it took that long to dry. It hangs in my living room to this day.

The eggs in LA

When you talk about the best eggs, that's when I think of Los Angeles. Not long ago, I went to Los Angeles to do a screen test. Hurrah, I thought. So many Brits have done so well in American films and for years I have been filled with jealousy, for I am indeed a very jealous person. I had noticed there was a shortage of old women in films, particularly since the wonderful Ruth Gordon went, and had thought, well, there must be a little spot for me.

So here I was. Stepping off a Virgin flight massaged, manicured, and full of champagne and good food. I was met by a stretch limo. I don't know how long

(L.A. AIRPORT)

I was met by a stretch limo.

they normally are, but this one was stretched to full length. The driver was very proud of it.

I settled at the back and took the long view. The floor was covered wall to wall with black shag-pile carpet. The fitful rays creeping through the darkened windows lit the sad, dusty tufts, which gave the appearance of having had a hard life. Fastened to the back was a wire shelf

201

supporting a row of melancholy bottles made of some sort of synthetic glass, which even had the cheek to flaunt marks like engraved crystal. Inside the bottles, some very dubious liquids wobbled and burped. The final touch was the vases of curled-up plastic flowers arranged at regular intervals around the roof.

I arrived at the Four Seasons Hotel, where I lived in great splendour for a few days. Then I took myself off to a very nice quiet hotel called Shangri-la right on the front at Santa Monica, where I had a room with a kitchen and a view of the sea.

My friend Sue had come and driven me around until we found this place. Sue was my grandson Tom's first nanny. She had married an American and now lived in LA. It was lovely to see her again, and my visit there would have been much lonelier without her.

There was a big garden just outside my room where I could sit and eat or read, or watch the humming-birds suck nectar out of exotic flowers.

Life was full of wig-fittings, wardrobe and so on. The palm trees, shading a long walk in front of the sea, looked pretty from across the road. Unfortunately, I was going through one of those times when I feel unnaturally tired; I have suffered from these exhausting spells for forty years now. What this means is when I go for a walk I have to sit down along the way.

There were plenty of seats all along the seafront, but when I went to sit down I found that every one was occupied by a heap of rags with a sleeping body inside it. I tried giving a dollar to one heap, and a hand shot out to grab it like something from an Egyptian tomb, with long, filthy claws.

So I tried to make my way on to the beach. I didn't find it easy, and when I got there, it was too big. There was no friendly person to hire me a deckchair to sit in. I felt lost. The sea was miles away. It would have been fine had I been on a bike or a pair of skates, but I was just an old girl who wanted to sit and look at the sea. It was not my kind of beach. But it was beautiful to watch the sunset from the roof of the Shangri-la Hotel.

My main joy was to go every night and wander up and down the pedestrianized streets nearby. I loved those streets. They were busy all day long, and as night wore on they became even more lively.

The shops and cafés were open until all hours. Plenty of seats and plenty to entertain. Singers and bands and performers of every kind gave their all to the audience passing by. The place had that lovely swirl of humanity that is universal, whether in Covent Garden, Paris or Marrakesh, or in Ben Jonson's *Bartholomew Fair*. Youngsters stood on their heads or twinkled their toes or played on their trumpets or grouped together in a band,

and someone else would sit on a stool and draw your portrait for a coin, tell your fortune, or just sell you a string of beads.

I really enjoy places like that – they make me feel part of the human race. The shops were a good mixture, too. I even found one that sold Scottish oatmeal. I never expected to find that there, but I did, and was able to make my porridge which I have every morning.

In LA, the farmers' market came twice a week to the street beside the Shangri-la Hotel. It was a long street packed from end to end with stalls selling the most delicious, delectable, mouthwatering food, all grown by the people who presented it so proudly.

I would come back to the hotel laden with avocados, onions, raspberries, beetroot, nuts and dried fruit. Oh, and the eggs! I have never had eggs like that. I bought them from a stall where they showed you the daily diet of their hens – a combination of the most nutritious food you can give them. Now I had the little kitchen, I could cook my own food.

Do you know, after five weeks, the job fizzled out. It can happen. In fact, you never can tell you have got a job until you've done it – and sometimes not even then, because despite spending months on it, you, or it, may not be shown.

So I crept back, jobless, on to the plane, having been taken to the airport this time in a very ordinary taxi. But if you say 'Los Angeles' to me, I can say with all my heart, 'The boiled eggs are lovely.'

Gran's legacy

Any cooking skills I have must have been absorbed from my Gran. She never consciously taught me, but I suppose I picked up some basic feeling about food.

Because of seeing her cook, I have never had scales or measured anything – just throw it in a bowl. And so it passes on through the generations because my daughter is a brilliant cook, without scales but with the same movement of her hand, bashing flour around in a bowl, that Gran had. When I see her table set for a meal, I am filled with mouthwatering, uncontrollable greed.

When I was a child, we never had sauce in a bottle. Roast beef meant digging the horseradish from the garden, then the agonizing task of shredding it to make a sauce that lifted the top off your head and made you gasp for breath.

These days I take a short cut and get my horseradish

ground in cute little jars from Fortnum's. Not that I put it on beef now, but it's lovely on salmon or smoked trout.

Lots of things I don't eat now, but can still feel the taste in my mouth. For instance, on a cold winter's night, to have calves' brains on toast for tea. The idea of eating calves' brains now fills me with horror, yet I can still feel the creaminess on my tongue with a sprinkling of white pepper.

The smoothness of marrow scraped out of a bone.

The black inkiness of the juice running out of wild mushrooms. Where has that taste gone? They all taste like cardboard now.

Hot oven-bottom bread and cakes torn open, running with butter and syrup, to be eaten greedily.

Lobster, with only a squeeze of lemon and a dusting of cayenne. Alas, I cannot face them any more, now that I have sat on the seafront at Brighton and seen them being boiled in a pot.

TV gold

The Vicar of Dibley must be one of the most popular, most loved series ever. Of all the people who stop me in the street, nearly all still want to talk about *Dibley* and how much they enjoyed it – many watch it over and over again. They constantly quote the doings of the character I played, the lady who made the cakes. Those cakes were packed with the most disgusting things, put there in all innocence and from a desire to do good, but poison to the tastebuds. Things like Branston Pickle or sardines in chocolate cake.

My character, Letitia Cropley, was a truly great invention and has welded itself into the minds of viewers. What can I say about making the series? – except that all I can remember is chocolate. Chocolate everywhere.

Cakes, buns, chocolate slabs, biscuits, chocolate-coated this and that. Chocolate every day. Dawn French loves chocolate, and wherever you went there it was and you could help yourself and eat as much as you liked.

Mrs Cropley became such an established figure that I was utterly shocked when I received the script for the episode that contained her death. Poor Mrs Cropley died of a heart attack one Easter, and people who stop me in the street still mourn her passing. It's not the same without the terrible cakes, they say.

As one lady in Liberty's said to me, 'Did you really die?' But far better was to come.

That old sofa

One day, a little script slipped through the letter box, unannounced. No one had said a word about it coming, as if it was not important enough to mention. It was called *The Royle Family*. My heart glows as I write those words. What can I say about *The Royle Family* that has not been said a thousand times?

It turned comedy-watching on its head – in fact, some people said it was not comedy. It was the brilliant creation of Caroline Aherne and Craig Cash.

Most of the action took place on the sofa in the living room, with all the family lined up watching television. To sit there, on that sofa, squashed like sardines, was simply heaven and felt just like being in a real family. Caroline and Craig were the writers, but they sat on the sofa with everyone else. It was their creation, their show, but they expected no star treatment. A lot of people would have wanted special shots, special angles, special everything. But Caroline and Craig just got on with it, like the rest of us.

I think Sue Johnston has never given a finer perform-ance than she gave as that mother, a put-upon and cheerful slave to her family. *As her* mother, I was a selfish old bag who expected her to wait on me. I remember in one scene holding up a toffee paper, after I had eaten the toffee, for her to take away.

Of course, Ricky Tomlinson was the archetypal lazy dad who did nothing but sit in his chair – he was the only one *not* on the sofa – and watch television and bicker with me.

Everything about it was different. For a start, there was no audience. No mass of people to hide from behind a screen until the warm-up man had finished, then come running out flashing smiles all round. No audience to play to – and no doubt give an over-emphasis in some places just because they were there. It was played in a completely naturalistic way, which to some people seemed as if we were improvising.

But improvise we did not. Not a bit of it. Every word was very strictly scripted. If just one word was altered it was settled upon by Caroline and Craig together. Hand-held cameras caught every utterance, and the editing by Tony Cranstoun was perfect.

Ralf Little gave up his medical studies to be the son of the family, always expected to make the tea. The nextdoor neighbours were divinely played by Doreen Keogh, Peter Martin and Jessica Stevenson, who became the co-writer of her own series called *Spaced*.

You can see that I consider *The Royle Family* to be a

highlight in my career, and I think that applies to most of us who were in it.

I was very lucky to have that experience.

A delightful confection

Roald Dahl must be one of the most popular authors in the world. So when Tim Burton takes one of his stories to film, well, that's a double whammy. When Tim was planning *Charlie and the Chocolate Factory*, I found I was to be one of the grandparents sharing the bed in Charlie's little old cottage.

The first day on the set, the four grandparents were taken on a grand tour. It was unbelievable, what they had set up for that film. I have never seen a set like it: streets of houses, rivers of chocolate, valleys of beautiful trees hanging with lollipops. What would audiences think of the squirrels? Real ones, taught to open nuts. Can you believe it?

As to our little cottage, it was all for real and so amazingly planned. The floor was so steep and so broken, us old ones – well, this old one – had to be led by the hand across it and on to the great old bed. Once there, on the bed, we could relax for the scene. What a way to earn a living, I used to think each day. Taken out to studios in the countryside, then undress, get into a nightdress and climb into bed. And with very nice companions too – the other grandparents were very chatty.

My hands didn't quite know what to do, so I took my crochet and managed to do quite a long scarf. I crocheted my hat as well.

The cottage got a bit of a battering during the course of the story. But it was all done for real, there were no false effects, and it was quite something to see the glass elevator come crashing through the roof, to land at our bedside. And inside, just standing there, only a few inches away from us, the gorgeous Johnny Depp.

What about the scrumptious Johnny? I mean to say, that isn't something that happens every day. It had never happened to me before. Unfortunately.

And it was a privilege to work with an inspired director like Tim Burton and be welcomed on to the set by him. What a joy!

Cornish pride

While writing this book, I have been down to Cornwall to do a popping-up part in a film called *Keeping Mum*. I know it will be popular. It's a black comedy written and directed by Niall Johnson with a cast including Maggie Smith, Kristin Scott Thomas, Rowan Atkinson and Patrick Swayze. What a roll-call. Wow! It was lovely to see Maggie Smith again, after twenty years, when I played her mother in *A Private Function*.

I had never been to Cornwall before and must confess I did find it a bit hilly and steep. But the place that was used for the location was like something lost in time. It was in the midst of a maze of tiny lanes and consisted of no more than a handful of cottages, a vicarage and a church and about twenty inhabitants. I have never seen so many trees, except in the forests of Czechoslovakia. It was all positively feudal.

I enjoyed the trip and it was good to be by the sea for a few weeks. I was lucky enough to be in Falmouth when Dame Ellen MacArthur came in from her trip around the world. I stood and cheered with the others when she came out and danced on her boat. This was the day after she had arrived, but the crowds were still all there to welcome her. I go all misty-eyed and bursting with pride when I look on a scene like that, and she was so pleasant and unassuming about it all – that made her even more endearing.

I go silly, too, when I'm on an aeroplane and they announce: 'Fasten your seatbelts, we are about to arrive at Heathrow.' Oh heavens, I practically kiss the earth like the old Pope used to do.

I never feel safe, wherever I have been, until that moment.

Home comforts

I no longer live in the old haunted house backing on to the forest. I have moved a lot since those days – in fact, I have grown to like moving. Each time I get the feeling that this time it will be a little bit better. It's a characterless house that I live in now, but it's full of light and that I love. There are no ghosts here.

I am writing some of this on the roof, where I spend a lot of time on a good day. I'm up with the tops of the trees that surround, and from here I can see right over Hampstead Heath and the spires of Alexandra Palace on the other side.

There are lots of birds to watch. Big fat pigeons, smart, unloved magpies, little thrushes, sparrows, the odd robin, the character-actor blackbird. Squirrels leap from roof to tree and dart in and steal the breadcrumbs when I put them out for the birds. There are butterflies and bees and wasps, and the occasional red medical helicopter lowering down to pick someone up off the Heath.

But one of the most stunning sights is to see a group of swans, their long necks outstretched, flying towards the ponds on the heath. They look like a fleet of Concordes.

Back to Brighton

I always enjoy a trip to the sea when I can get there. Recently, I found myself in my favourite spot opposite the West Pier. It was looking more beautiful than it has ever been.

I sat there with the throngs of people enjoying the seaside on a day that turned out to be unnaturally hot. As usual I wallowed in the heat under the yellow beach umbrella, feeling quite protected from the sun.

To my dismay later that evening, though, I saw in the mirror that my face was the colour of a Victorian chest of drawers. It was on fire. In my youth, I had foolishly overexposed myself to the sun in order to become instantly brown, but I hadn't felt like this before.

What to do? All I could think of was to soak a face flannel in cold water and wear it on the hot spots. I had breakfast in my room rather than face the crowds, but decided later to make for the seafront. Pulling a straw hat low over my face, I crawled along at a dismal pace, feeling deeply sorry for myself. Slowly it entered my head that what I needed was a cucumber to slice and press down on my hot skin.

All around me were happy crowds enjoying the sunshine, dashing here and there on bikes or skates, or strolling along. I noticed a group of three on their way to the beach. It was obvious that this bunch were going to eat a lot, for they were hung about with huge quantities of food.

I carefully noted the shape of the foodie things showing through their thin supermarket bags, then, to my surprise, I saw that one bag had a little hole in the base and sticking out was six inches of cucumber. The trio shot down to the sea edge and when I reached the spot where they had been, the cucumber was lying on the sand at my feet.

Three people were running down
to the edge of the sea.

Mrs Mulch

I have loved Wallace and Gromit ever since I saw *The Wrong Trousers*, so of course I was very pleased to do a voice in their big film, *The Curse of the Were-Rabbit*.

My character is Mrs Mulch and she is a very earthy creature whose passion in life is growing prize pumpkins.

Recording the voice was just like no other job. It may be only one line at a time, yet it might have to be repeated a thousand times in order to fit the movement of that plasticine mouth.

Nick Park and Steve Box are a treat to work with. They are so casual; you just cannot believe they are building such a huge film.

Water Aid

I have been very lucky to be involved with some fantastic charities. My first experience was when I went with SAGE to the Chelsea Flower Show. Help the Aged used to have a garden at the show, specially designed and entered for the competition. It was always a beautiful garden, and came very high in the voting stakes.

Anyway, they liked to have, as part of the presentation, various members of SAGE pottering about in the garden or sitting in the shed, chattering away, maybe having a cup of tea, even smiling at any photographer that happened to be around.

This particular day was very hot – it really was a heat wave – and all very tiring. In fact, my feet were killing me. So I made my way down the path, took a side turning and found a seat under some beautiful shady trees. Here I was able to take my shoes off and, in the haze of the warm afternoon and the far-off buzz of everything, have a little doze, which is essential to my nature.

Then, into the shady space walked two taps, two full-blown kitchen taps. They were also seeking a quiet moment. The tops of the taps lifted up and out popped two lovely girls, Jules and Hannah. They were from Water Aid, a charity they were promoting at the show, which aims to make clean water available to everyone in the world. A splendid charity, when you remember how we turn on taps and use clean water all the time without thinking about it. Yet too many people still have to walk for miles for a bucketful and have nothing but filthy pond water to drink.

We got chatting, and when they asked me if I could come in on their next campaign I said I would be very pleased to.

And that is how I came to be sitting in the middle of Covent Garden on a lavatory.

I sat there for several hours, holding a newspaper that had headlines screaming at the world: 'Toilets for all by 2025!', then peering through a lavatory seat saying the same thing. The girls stood alongside me, rigged up as lavatories and with a cleaning brush coming out of the tops of their heads.

We got some wonderful pictures. But nobody stopped to look. Nobody gave us a second glance. It was too ordinary for words, I suppose.

Just as we were packing up, a man all of a sweat came tearing along. He had heard on the radio that we were going to be there on call, and had rushed all the way from Tooting. 'You're too late, mate,' we said.

Whiskers on kittens

I have a deep love for animals and enjoy going to cat shows. At many I have been a cat judge. No, I don't know all the finer points of a pure-bred cat, all I know are the moggies. Usually I just have to judge the one with the longest tail or the pinkest nose or the sweetest smile.

It's terrible having to choose, because of the imploring looks of the owners standing nearby. There can only be one winner, but there are so many runners-up at a moggie show, they all get a rosette to pin on their cage or basket.

So you have the cats, in their cages, in the middle of the hall, with people circulating around them, pressing their faces against the wire and cooing and oohing and aahing at the sight of such loveliness.

Then, all around the edge of the hall are the stalls. Each stall is presented by some animal welfare group and each sells its own thing. Some have homegrown fruit or jewellery or books. The tombola. The ever popular cake stall. My favourite one is the knitted stuff – the astonishing things that people are able to knit! Animals, people, houses – you name it, they will knit it. A lot of old ladies, housebound, can sit and knit an amazing assortment of things. I love dolls and dolls' clothes knitted by them, with tiny socks and shoes and hats and little frocks under little coats. I have a doll that sits on my bed with one sock missing. My grandson had fun dressing and undressing her when he was two years old. Soon he will be thirty.

I have some medals knitted by some old lady I consider to be real fashion statements. Someday I will go somewhere with them pinned to my chest and no doubt will get a fashion mention in a magazine.

So today I am patron of a cat sanctuary way down in a quiet country lane in Kent, called the Rhodes Minnis Cat Sanctuary. Once a year they have an open day and that is quite an event.

A hired bus crawls around north London, picking us up at various points, and takes us down to this little lane just outside Folkestone. The chatter on the bus is all about cats and dogs, how many cats this person or that has taken in. Some have twenty or more.

The stalls are full of the lovely things usually found on stalls, but being in Kent there's a stall of Kentish honey too, and meringues made from the eggs from the farm next door, where the hens roam free. If you were a stray cat you would want to be given a home there.

The sanctuary was started by one Veronica J. Huthwaite in 1970. She lived in a small bungalow with a lot of land behind it, and her own personal cats lived with her and the strays spread out behind. When she died, she left 102 personal cats. Fortunately, the place was taken over by trustees, who have cared for and improved it until it is a treat to go there for the day.

It has paved walks and flowerbeds, and sitting places to talk to the cats. There is a sick bay and a kittenry, and a place for older cats to sit and snooze on wool blankets knitted especially for them. There is a space for feral cats too, who do not care to look for homes but are content to just feel safe and fed, and they can still lie in the sun or shelter out of the rain.

So all of us twittering humans move around eating our ice-cream and the Kentish meringues that leave sugar on our lips. We swoon at the sight of the kittens playing in the kittenry, and are silenced with respect for the lady who has brought her special cats that she takes to hospitals and old people's homes for the residents to stroke. We buy tickets for the tombola, and plants and home-made cakes, and win bottles of whisky with raffle tickets. When it's time to leave, we pack into the bus to come home, laden with our purchases. Plants take up a lot of room, so there's much shifting about to fit things in. Someone has found a cat they couldn't leave behind and has adopted it on the spot. Its mewing mixes with the chatter.

The weather has been kind. Only a couple of drizzles, with sunshine in between, a typical summer's day. Mary comes round with an envelope to collect tips for the driver. Someone asks him to wait a minute, she's forgotten to buy some of the very fresh eggs from the farm next door. Finally, the bus heads back to London, and several people fall asleep.

A very English day.

Jimmy the donkey

This morning, the postman brought me a letter from Jimmy. Enclosed with it was his latest photograph, and he's as handsome as ever. Jimmy is a pure white donkey living at a home for distressed donkeys in Wadebridge, Cornwall.

Jimmy came into my life when I was a guest on Graham Norton's TV show. I had just been appearing in *The Royle Family* so was treated like a royal. They put a jewelled crown on my head, then I was seated on a throne and carried down into the audience by some gorgeous boys.

Graham is such enormous fun because he is a very easy person to work with. And it's a naughty show, but whereas some hosts might make it sound dirty, Graham's surprised expression into the camera turns anything risqué into innocence. So it was lots of fun, and my gift at the end of the show was to adopt a donkey for a year.

A fine time

I have been fortunate in finding a career I have loved. Acting has given me so many opportunities and friends, as well as visits to interesting places. Looking back, the variety has been enjoyable, and you just do not know what will come next.

These days I like to sit in my chair, dreaming and thinking of all the things I should be doing. Now I have quite a splendid chair. I bought it in Harrods and it's upholstered as a chair should be. Throw yourself into it, and you float.

Well, I spend an awful lot of time in that chair. I'm welded to it. Staring into space or maybe nodding off. I like a bit of music in the background. Nearly every day I play Al Bowlly. I like the old songs and their words.

But the greatest happiness is my family. Having missed out on brothers and sisters in my youth, it's a joy to have two children and four grandchildren. They stand high as trees and I stand by them like a little old bush. Thank goodness for a family. One of the greatest moments of my life is to see them seated all together around the dining table. Gran and Grandad would be proud.

Picture credits

Liz Smith owns the copyright in all the pictures in this book except for the following which are courtesy of:

BFI: 7
BBC: 11, 22
David Farrell: 12
LWT: 13
Paragon Entertainment: 14, 15
Radio Times: 19
Eric Tabisz: 25
ITV: 26
Empics: 28
Robert Smith: 29, 30

The publishers have made every effort to contact copyright holders in the pictures reproduced in this book. Where this has not been possible the publishers will be happy to hear from anyone who recognises their material.

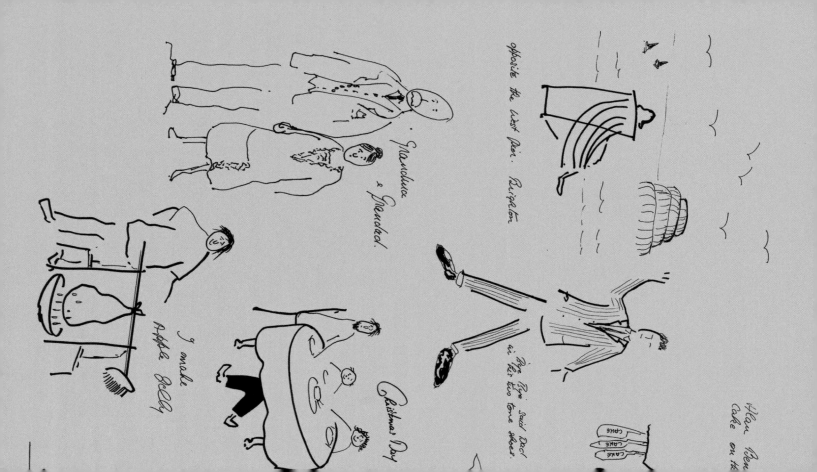